More praise fo

"Branding is the single m[...]
cept today. . . . Readers using Andrusia and [...]
branding suggestions will stand head and shoulders above
the rest. For people in any field, this book is a must and an
idea whose time has truly come."
> —Doug Gleason, Senior Vice President, Marketing
> MGM Consumer Products

"This idea is brilliant! A step-by-step guide to finding your
unique talents, enhancing them and embracing them . . .
Readers who follow the authors' advice will rise to the top
and become visible anywhere. I can tell if someone is branded
the minute they enter a room."
> —Michael Levine, Search Consultant

"This is an idea whose time has come. In today's environment, branding yourself is every bit as important as your education and experience. David Andrusia and Rick Haskins are
the perfect teachers."
> —Stewart Fine, Vice President, Marketing
> Alberto-Culver

"Finally someone understands that it takes more than an education to make your mark. Creating a unique niche for yourself is creating lifelong employment for yourself. Clever idea!"
> —Laurence Taylor, Former President
> Vidal Sassoon Haircare
> Executive Consultant
> Donna Karan

"Times have never been tougher for graduating students, but
those who use the authors' branding techniques will stand
out in the crowd. This is a guide that gets people not just a
job, rather it helps them to forge an identity that lands them
the job of their dreams."
> —Greg Ptacek
> Author of *The 150 Best Companies for Liberal Arts
> Graduates*

Also by David Andrusia

THE PERFECT PITCH
How to Sell Yourself for Today's Job Market

BRAND YOURSELF

How to Create an Identity for a Brilliant Career

DAVID ANDRUSIA AND RICK HASKINS

BALLANTINE BOOKS • NEW YORK

A Ballantine Book
Published by The Ballantine Publishing Group

www.randomhouse.com/BB/

Library of Congress Cataloging-in-Publication Data
Andrusia, David.
Brand yourself : how to create an identity for a brilliant career /
David Andrusia and Rick Haskins. — 1st ed.
p.   cm.
ISBN 0-345-42359-3 (tr : alk. paper)
1. Success in business.   2. Career development.   3. Self-presentation.
4. Business names.   I. Haskins, Rick.   II. Title.
HF5386.A5737   1999
650.1—dc21   98-43541
CIP

Cover design by Heather Kern

Manufactured in the United States of America
First Edition: January 2000
10   9   8   7   6   5   4   3

You're any kind of man you damn well want to make yourself.
—Steven Millhauser,
  Martin Dressler: The Tale of an American Dreamer

If you follow the herd, you will simply get branded with the rest.
—David Andrusia's horoscope, August 31, 1997,
  The New York Post

CONTENTS

David Andrusia thanks: Rick Haskins, the ultimate brand guru; Katharine Sands, who believed in this project from the start, and valiantly kept it on track; everyone at Ballantine, especially Ellen Archer, Maureen O'Neal, Joni Rendon, and—biggest thank-you of all!—Elizabeth Zack, an editor whose talent and kindness know no peer. Kudos to Doug Grad, who acquired the book and made it a "go." Big kiss to my friends and family.

Rick Haskins thanks: My former bosses and colleagues, who taught me; my coauthor David Andrusia; Doug Grad and Joni Rendon, who captured the vision; Maureen O'Neal and Elizabeth Zack, who expertly executed it; Katharine Sands, my agent, mentor, and occasional afternoon tea partner; and my entire family, who always support me in everything I do.

You, Inc.

Why You Need to Brand Yourself for Career Success

Career coaches. Professional seminars. On-line job chats. And, of course, books like this one, which you've very kindly bought.

Twenty years ago, when we graduated from college, there were nowhere near the number of career boosters that exist today. And there's a reason why this has changed. Despite what politicians tell us about job growth, the competition for positions in all fields is fiercer than ever before. We'll spare you the macroeconomic analysis; the key reasons for this hypercompetitiveness are:

- a greater number than ever before of college-educated women and men
- corporate downsizing, begun in the '80s, and continuing today
- consolidation and takeovers of companies is reducing the workforce considerably, a trend that will continue well into the millennium
- automation and computerization that has reduced the number of human bodies required in many industries and fields

Think about your own career or those of family and friends: don't you know at least one person who has been affected by the societal and economic factors mentioned on page one? And, if you're to be perfectly honest with yourself, hasn't your own career path been a bit more tortuous than you might once have believed?

This is why, dear reader, you have to find a way to stand out from the crowd . . . why *you have to brand yourself if you are to achieve optimal career success.*

Let us be very clear. You can hope and pray that you'll rise to the top by sheer dint of your merits and good work alone. Perhaps, in the best of all possible worlds, that is how things would work. But in the hypercompetitive atmosphere of today's retrenched times, you need to do far more than that to make the most out of your career—wherever you are, whatever your field.

That is why we have developed a business helping people like you find their personal brands, and it is why we are writing this book. Whether you are a corporate accountant or a dental hygienist, a computer technician or a budding entrepreneur, *Brand Yourself* lets you use the same proven principles we teach in our career seminars to achieve sterling success in your chosen profession.

And here's more good news: branding yourself works wonderfully for the new and recent graduate, too. In fact, helping first-timers get the jobs of their dreams is among the most rewarding work we do.

Why is having a brand so important? Because in just a few words, through one image—and, ideally, by its very name— a brand conveys to consumers a strong, positive sense of a product or service, and why it is different and better than the competition. Most important of all, a strong brand image impels people to *buy*. This has been a proven strategy in the world of advertising and marketing for decades. Many young product managers employed at blue-chip packaged-goods firms have no intention of spending a lifetime devising brand strategies for shampoo or barbecue sauce, but by learning how to create marketing programs for these admittedly mundane items, they know they will have mastered the coveted art of forging brand identities for any product or service—anytime, anywhere.

Branding is such a powerful tool in selling products that it makes perfect sense that we as individuals should brand ourselves—thereby creating a strong, positive sense of ourselves (the product) and our services that is different and better than what our peers have to offer (the competition)—for the greatest possible career success. Remember: in advertising, a strong brand image propels people to buy—so in terms of you and your career, this means *hire, promote*, and, yes, endorse or buy the services you have to offer.

Many high-profile people in a vast range of fields already have done this, although nowhere is it more apparent than in the entertainment industry, where branding—though it was never called that until now—has been a de facto force for decades. Joan Crawford was the gruff, gritty broad who got her man no matter what obstacles were thrown in her way; Rudolph Valentino romanced as the Latin lover; Kate Hepburn played an accessible American aristocrat to the hilt; and Cary Grant formed a memorable brand as a suave-yet-bumbling leading man. In the past ten years the entertainment industry has come to be even less about artistic achievement and more about product and marketing. Why does Julia Roberts get more than $20 million per picture? It's because she has become a product that sells movie tickets through her nervous laughter, megawatt smile, and terrific Titian hair. Mainstream audiences of all ages find Julia utterly endearing in her dizzy, romantic comedy roles, and for this box office allure, studio execs are willing to pay her big bucks.

Indeed, Julia Roberts has branded herself beautifully as a sassy, smart (but less than brainiac), and sexy romantic lead. That, in a phrase, is her personal branding statement (something you'll begin to develop once you get to chapter two). Note, too, that when she deviates from this brand—as in the turgid *Mary Reilly* or Tinker Bell in *Hook*—her fans deviate from her. Yes, brands can be changed (as you'll find in chapter seven), but we'll show you why you'd better think twice before changing a successful one.

But branding is certainly not only for stars of film. It is for:

- *Brick,* an attorney with a prestigious old-line law firm—the kind of top-drawer institution attracting clients by dint of its reputation alone. But Brick wanted to stand apart from his colleagues, so he actively solicited new business. He conducted a direct-mail campaign using his prep school, college, and law school directories, plus the membership rosters of several blue-chip clubs. Soon he was known at his firm as "the guy who brought $2 million in new bookings to the firm last year." Is it a surprise Brick made partner before anyone else from his law school class?

- *Shandra,* a secretary who wanted to break away from the pack. She surveyed her competition and saw that they treated their positions as "just a job." Savvy Shandra amassed topflight computer skills, started dressing in a professional way, and began to greet top executives by name. Soon she became known as "the computer whiz who knows everyone in the company and is the most stylish person in the firm." Shandra has branded herself brilliantly . . . and is now working as the executive assistant to the head of the company!

• *Jonelle,* an independent accountant who had been searching for a way to make her service the best in town. She decided that what people really wanted was to know the "why" behind the numbers—and started to provide a written précis to each and every client, explaining what she had done in layman's terms. Suddenly she became "the accountant who puts the numbers in perspective"—a great tag for brochures and the press—and found herself with 75 percent more clients than the previous year.

• *Alejandro,* an aerobics instructor who saw that his class easily tired of the same old routines. He created a totally new aerobics approach and in short order, everyone in the gym wanted to take his class. Alejandro bestowed a new name upon what he was teaching—"Alerobics"—and alerted the press. He soon became L.A.'s newest fitness guru, and now has an infomercial of his own. Alejandro branded himself as a name to be recognized—and reckoned with—in his field.

HOW THIS BOOK WILL HELP YOU SUCCEED

The ultimate goal of branding yourself is so that you can stand head and shoulders higher than your competition— to get you noticed by your boss (as Brick did), by a new employer (as Shandra did), or by the clients you seek (as with Jonelle and Alejandro). In other words, we want you to become a star in your field, and branding yourself helps you achieve just that, whether you're seeking to climb the corporate ladder higher than where you are; are looking for a new position in the same field or different industry; or want to promote your business or yourself.

But there's a wonderful side benefit, too, an extra added bonus that following the advice in this book will bring. And that is this: *you'll find out what you really love to do, and your work becomes not only more profitable, but more rewarding as well.* That's because, as you'll soon see, identifying not only your skills but your *passions* is a key component of developing your brand.

WHO WE ARE

Both of us spent our twenties and early thirties as marketeers with blue-chip firms, so branding as a business strategy is something we know. David was an executive at Revlon, Swatch Watch USA, and New Line Cinema, and Rick is an alumnus of Procter & Gamble, Vidal Sassoon, and The Walt Disney Company. Both of us were known as iconoclasts — guys with creative ideas who cared more about blazing new paths than about toeing the corporate line and "playing the part." That, as you can guess, is why we both eventually went out on our own as consultants and writers for established companies and developing firms in a wide range of fields.

In any case, both of us were known for our expertise in landing great jobs with hot firms, and so had long been asked by friends and acquaintances to help plan their own job searches. Then, in 1995, David wrote a book called *The Perfect Pitch: How to Sell Yourself in Today's Job Market*, which was published to excellent reviews two years later. Inspired by the positive reaction to his book, David started giving seminars and began a private practice as a career coach.

Rick, who had just left Disney and was working as an independent TV producer and marketing consultant, offered all the encouragement you'd expect a friend to give. Then, a couple months after the book's publication, he offered some specific advice: "Your book's great for people who know what they're after, but there's a whole group of folks out there who can't pitch themselves, because they don't know who they are, what they're best at, and what kind of job they want."

"True enough," David agreed. "What are you suggesting?"

"Well, think about this. What do all of the supersuccessful people we know have in common? They can all describe who they are and what they do better than anyone else in twenty-five words or less. People can identify them in just a few words."

"Yes, you're right. . . ."

"Well, what do we call a product with an instantly recognizable identity?"

"A brand, of course," David offered, beginning to see what Rick was getting to.

"So shouldn't people have their own brand if they are to stand out from the pack and be as visible and successful as possible in their careers?"

Yes, they should, we agreed, and the concept for *Brand Yourself* was born. In fact, even before this book was bought by a publisher, much less brought into print, we began giving seminars on self-branding and incorporating these potent, career-building ideas into our private practice.

Now you, too, can learn the step-by-step ways to brand yourselves that we teach clients and career seminar attendees:

- how to formulate your own Personal Branding Statement by analyzing your best skills, passions, and market needs
- how to rebrand yourself for a new job or career
- how to package your brand to reflect its attributes

- how to broadcast your brand—to your boss, a new employer, prospective clients, and/or the world at large
- how to perfect your brand to attain the ultimate possible career success

In the past few years, we've helped many people in every imaginable field brand themselves for success. You, too, can use this program to realize your professional goals. Standing out among the crowd is the key to long-term success, and the time to begin is *now*.

But before rushing headlong into our branding system, we invite you to take a brief tour of the history of the brand as a marketing force. Turn the page, and begin to understand why branding is so important, and what having a brand can do for you.

CHAPTER ONE

Maximum Impact

The Power of a Brand

Crest. *Cheer.* Colgate.

Palmolive. Pontiac. ***Pert Plus.***

Ajax. AIR FRANCE. Airborne Express.

Fifty percent of Americans don't know who their congressman is, but we'd bet 95 percent of us have heard the names above.

Now, quick: what do all of these have in common? Alliteration, yes, but something else besides . . . something that companies around the world spend billions of dollars to create, and every business would give its eyeteeth to have.

If you guessed "products," you're only halfway there. Of course, all of these are tangible commodities—except Air France and Airborne Express, which are, strictly speaking, services—but so are the generic detergents, no-name toothpastes, and the unmarked soap you just used at the gym.

What sets all of the above consumer products or services apart is the elusive, much-sought-after quality that their names possess. Each of them is a *brand*.

THE POWER OF A BRAND

What is a brand? It's a way of encapsulating and communicating a product's power, pitch, and position in the most succinct way: the combination of one name and visual image—a *personality*—that anyone, anywhere, will recognize and interpret in precisely the same way.

The proof:

- BMW is the "ultimate driving machine"
- J. Crew signals "preppy-but-cool"
- Charmin is "squeezably soft"
- Hallmark is for "when you care enough to send the very best"
- AT&T lets you "reach out and touch someone"
- Yahoo asks, "Do you Yahoo?"

Why are companies so eager to brand their products and services? Because before spending millions of dollars on advertising, publicity, and sales promotion campaigns, marketing gurus want to make absolutely certain that there is a shared, unique, and preemptive positioning for the product they seek to sell. In short, they must define:

- the product's visual image
- the market it seeks to capture
- the unique product benefit(s) the competition lacks

before spending one cent to raise consumer awareness of the brand. Why even bother to advertise a new toothpaste until you know what makes it different from and better than Crest?

How pervasive is the power of the brand? It is so great that even in ostensibly communist China people will pay a month's wages for the supposedly life-enhancing experience of eating a Big Mac. That, in a phrase, is the ultimate goal of branding: *to create a product or service people think they just can't live without.*

In today's world, we are inundated by thousands of "brand messages" every day. Branding has become such an integral part of our existence that phrases like "You deserve a break today" are no longer mere slogans; they have become the subliminal mantras guiding our daily lives. This, of course, is the consumer marketing strategy of companies large and small: hear, see, internalize, motivate, buy.

Think we're overstating the case? That you're impervious to the brand messages we all receive? Then read this brand-consciousness challenge, and become aware of the nearly nonstop brand broadcasts we see and hear from dawn till dusk. If you're the average American, your day will begin something like this:

7:00 A.M. Your radio alarm goes off and the music blares. You press the snooze function, praying for a few minutes' more peace. The alarm sounds again. Now you stretch and contemplate the day ahead. And before you've been awake for a full minute, you hear your first brand messages of the day: a pod of three commercials strategically placed amid the deejay's would-be witty banter. You check your watch to see if it's really time to get up and—pow! in your face—get a second dose of branding: the Timex or Seiko logo on your watch's face.

7:15 A.M. You hop in the shower, get a whiff of your soap's scent, notice its color, and feel the name imprinted on the bar. You grab your shampoo, recognizing the product by its shape alone, and take in the pleasant smell. The fragrance and other features of these products are distinct, programmed aspects of its brand, all designed to elicit positive, sensuous feelings even before you're towel dried.

7:45 A.M. You dash out of the house, stop by the local McDonald's for an Egg McMuffin, eye a billboard for the new Disney movie, then hit the road. Traffic, to your great chagrin, is moving more slowly than some on-line connections. Bored, you let your eyes wander across the sea of cars, stuck like so many beached whales, and notice the brand emblazoned on every vehicle you see. You turn on the radio and hear more commercials. The brand hits keep coming at you. . . .

8:30 A.M. Once in the office, you turn on your Mac or Compaq, check AOL for e-mail messages, and call AT&T for phone messages. You have just processed a dozen more brand messages, all subliminally received by, and registered in, your brain.

9:00 A.M. The guy who delivers the coffee is sporting an MTV hat and a Nike shirt, and is whistling the theme of the new Pepsi ad. He asks if you'd like a Winchell's doughnut or the marginally more nutritious Balance bar. Back at your desk, you breeze through the newspaper, noting up to ten ads for products and services on nearly every page.

You've been up for only two hours and have already been accosted by hundreds—yes, hundreds—of brand messages. These are hardly songs you've sought out, but subtly, ever so subtly, these messages have wended their way into your life. Continue to exercise your newfound brand awareness for the rest of the day and you'll be amazed at how pervasive and intractable branding has become in our lives. Can you even imagine an existence without "something special in the air" or where things didn't go better with Coke?

Of course, it hasn't always been this way. In fact, given the time that has elapsed since man first trod across the Earth, the creation of brands is a relatively new phenomenon. According to marketing history, branding as a marketing tool officially was born in 1931 when Procter & Gamble set up individual business units for each of its products as a way of according them the full attention their management and promotion required. But long before then, changes in America's economic and social picture began taking shape—changes that would directly affect the birth of the brand.

A NEW CONSUMER SOCIETY

A friend of ours with a heart of gold and an importing company hired a recent Bulgarian emigrant to work at his firm. After three months he let the poor fellow go. "Petkov tried so hard," our friend admitted, "but he just didn't get the fundamentals of marketing. He just thought all products were the same, had the same value, and should be priced and promoted exactly alike."

"With good reason," we said with a laugh. "In Bulgaria, they are!"

And, until recently, in Poland, Hungary, and the erstwhile U.S.S.R. In those communist societies, goods were all alike and there were no such things as brands.

In fact, just a century ago in America, things were pretty much as they still are in ex-Soviet satellites today. Picture your typical frontierswoman trudging three miles to the general store, the only outpost for hundreds of miles. Sadie Lou didn't care if the soap she chose was Zest or Dove; she praised God that there was any soap at all! Even more tellingly, staples like rice and flour were purchased in huge sacks. Not only was the lack of a pretty package unimportant, but even the price didn't matter much: you paid what the dealer asked. (When you've got the only store in the county, there are no price wars.)

With the advent of the Industrial Revolution and concomitant mass production in 1770, slowly but surely all this began to change. New tools were at the hands of inventors and entrepreneurs. New ways of performing drudgery like laundry and sewing were being created (even if they were still a long way off from the way these tasks are done today). New processes for making soap and toothpaste became available. And with all of these developments, there came the basis of branding theory: now consumers had a choice. Indeed, the ability to choose among like items is what marketing is really all about.

Along with industrialization came automation—and with that, increased leisure time. In addition to labor-saving devices there were new labor ethics that allowed laborers to work only half days on Saturdays. Add to these factors increased prosperity, and the consequence was clear: a new consumer society was taking shape.

Increased leisure time meant more time to read. As this trend was complemented by quicker, faster, and more sophisticated print production techniques, the outcome was inevitable: more newspapers and magazines—and advertising. At the same time, public places of leisure were the perfect venues for posters—the forerunners of today's outdoor advertising on billboards, buses, and benches.

All these conditions surfaced and fermented to create the underpinnings of modern marketing as we know it today. Suddenly, merely manufacturing a product wasn't enough: telling consumers what the product would do for them—

and, more important, how it would change their lives—was absolutely key.

Last Names As Brand Names

Granted, in the early days of marketing, there were no multi-national corporations or megabusinesses with hundreds of brands under one roof. Quite the contrary was true: most products were manufactured and distributed by one small company or even one individual. Almost universally these inventors and entrepreneurs (hats off to these early marke-teers!) would simply use their names as the products'; and so, with Stetson hats and Gillette razors, the brand name was born.

Today, these men—and, yes, women—have been immor-talized by the products and services they created and named after themselves. In fact, as Ronald Hambleton writes in *The Branding of America*, the period between 1800 and 1925 was to become known as the richest period of name-giving in the history of the brand.

To be sure, these marketing pioneers didn't set out to create brands per se, but—usually for lack of a better idea—attached their last names to the products they'd invented. Yes, Virginia, there was a Louis Chevrolet, and there were also founding fathers of these brands:

- Singer (sewing machines)
- Borden (condensed milk)
- Steinway (pianos)
- Campbell (soups)
- Swift (meat packing)
- Hires (root beer)
- Kraft (cheese)
- Maytag (washing machine)

- Schick (electric razor)
- Westinghouse (electricity transmission systems)
- Dow (chemicals)
- Eastman (photographic film)
- Deere (plows)
- Remington (shavers)
- Pitney and Bowes (postage meters)
- Colt (revolvers)
- Smith and Wesson (guns)
- Goodyear (rubber)
- Ford (cars)
- [the Earl of] Cardigan (sweaters)
- Baker's (chocolate)
- Colgate (toothpaste)
- Du Pont (chemicals)

At some point, competition arose and the products these last names adorned were no longer the only products in their category. Yet through either the product's inherent qualities or through savvy marketing, these brand names—and the products they adorn—withstood the test of time.

Without knowing it, these inventors and manufacturers had become the first branders as well. But it would be several decades before brand marketing began in earnest.

The Creation of Brand Marketing

By the mid-1800s consumers started to have a choice. Whether they picked (as they say today on the Home Shopping Network) "the look or the price," people were able to buy the products that most appealed to them. It follows, of course, that entrepreneurs with the best ideas and most-liked products got richer faster than those with mediocre or less-loved items on the shelves. One-man operations became companies with hundreds of employees practically overnight. To grow their businesses, these companies began to expand their product lines. Steinway complemented his original kitchen piano with innovative new entries; thus, the concert, parlor, and baby grand pianos were born.

Not only were additional "like" products being manufactured, but whole new lines were rapidly being introduced. Colgate, for instance, was now selling not just soap, but dentifrice (toothpaste) as well. But these early days of marketing had their rocky moments, as companies soon discovered that new products needed their own unique personalities in the marketplace; they needed their own *brands*.

Furthermore, these young companies weren't really set up to accommodate different products, especially from a manufacturing point of view. Their expansion into new lines of products was in many cases a painful learning process, as newly successful entrepreneurs were thrust feetfirst into the role of running fast-expanding companies—and planning for long-term growth.

No company felt these growing pains more acutely than a Midwestern consumer goods company started by two immigrants named William Procter and James Gamble. Originally candle and soap makers, they set up their company, Procter & Gamble (now known to the world as "P & G") on the banks of the highly traveled Ohio River in Cincinnati. They soon had a thriving business shipping their early products—candles—up and down the river to numerous ports.

In 1878 the partners introduced a hard white soap they called—how's this for basic?—P & G White Soap. In 1879, in a stroke of absolute genius, they changed the product's name to Ivory soap to better convey the product's benefits through a beneficent, positive word association—perhaps the first, and certainly the longest lasting, use of imagery in the history of the brand. Interestingly, while other entrepreneurs continued to bestow their last names on the items they produced, Procter & Gamble started naming their products with common nouns—words that communicated the product's benefits by providing positive emotional associations that just happened to convey the product's attributes as well. This progressive thinking was nothing short of revolutionary, and is indicative of the marketing foresight for which P & G has since become known.

Their genius had, unfortunately, a temporarily negative effect on their company's own products: Ivory became such a mammoth seller that the company's other soaps began to suffer from lack of attention. In 1931, a savvy P & G manager saw that Camay (their second most popular soap) was, according to company lore, being hurt because of "too much Ivory thinking." He proposed a new system wherein each product would be operated as an individual business unit so that managers could concentrate on that brand's specific needs. The recommendation was accepted and—voilà!—in one stroke of brilliance, the brand management system was born.

It wasn't long before America saw the formation of other consumer goods companies mimicking P & G's proven strategic recipe for success. Companies such as General Foods and General Mills began to embrace the brand management system. At the same time, fewer brands began to carry the names of their inventors because companies held multiple entries in the same product category and needed to differentiate between them, and because brand names implying benefits spoke volumes to consumers (those merely bearing the name of the inventor or company head said far less).

Shifts in the Marketplace

With the invention of television, for the first time in history the vast majority of American consumers could receive a brand message that could be both heard (as was the case in radio) and seen (as in the print media). Most important of all, products could be demonstrated and their benefits conveyed by images of real human beings whose lives had been or were being transformed by the products they used.

Early radio and TV shows were named after their sponsors, begetting yet another brilliant branding technique. As Jim Weinstein, former executive vice president of Wells Rich Greene Advertising, comments, "Advertisers helped foster television technology by providing the programming for consumers to watch; television helped the advertisers by allowing them to get their message out in the most interesting and effective way in history."

Even for those of us too young to have seen the shows, names like *Kraft Music Hall,* the *Colgate Comedy Hour,* and *Texaco Star Theater* remain alive in broadcasting lore. And *Hallmark Hall of Fame* is still on the air. By sponsoring these shows, branders were given a built-in opportunity to show viewers nationwide how their products would bring glory and joy to their lives.

In fact, television soon became such a powerful vehicle to get a product message out to the consumer that manufacturers began to lose focus on what consumers wanted, and instead would introduce whatever they could invent, as fast as possible. A new mentality among consumer products companies emerged: flood the marketplace with as many new entries as possible; after all, some of them had to stick!

At the same time, distribution—that is, the retail store— was getting closer and closer to the consumer, and soon knew more about the customer than the manufacturers did. This shift of power resulted in distributors telling manufacturing firms what to produce. Large chains started charging stocking allowances to manufacturers before they could even place their goods on the shelves. What resulted was a total turnaround in which branding played second fiddle to the key instruments of distribution management and pricing policy.

More recently, though, the emergence of new media has thrown an unexpected wrench in the way brand managers have been broadcasting their messages. A once easily quantifiable medium became an enigmatic one: the three national networks faced competition first from scores of cable stations, then from three new networks (Fox, WB, and UPN). The audience splintered, media buys were all over the place, and reaching the customer via the traditional television advertising routes was no longer a sure thing. How to reach millions with a brand message when the media pie was divided into so many small slivers?

To counteract television's now less-than-all-encompassing role, marketeers sought whole new ways to broadcast their brands. Soon brand messages were everywhere. Sports events of all types, from golf tournaments to figure skating competitions, were sponsored by Prudential, Nike, and NutraSweet. Official New York City marathon T-shirts were emblazoned with the corporate logos of Citibank and Virginia Slims. Products were showing up in movies, and movies were being promoted in restaurants and stores. And everyone was fighting for a site on the World Wide Web. A new era of brand cross-promotion had emerged. No place was safe from a brand message, not even previously sacrosanct places like doctors' offices and schools.

The Lasting Power of Brands

Then, in 1993, Philip Morris made an announcement that shook the marketing world. Effective immediately, the price of Marlboro cigarettes would be lowered by forty cents. The strongest brand in the history of mankind (*Financial World* magazine estimated the Marlboro brand to have a net worth of $39 billion) would no longer be competing on its revered brand image, but on price.

This maverick marketing strategy had its day in the sun, but after the dust cleared, it was obvious that branding was here to stay. While price did indeed influence purchase, it became clear it was not always or even sometimes the major variable at work in eliciting product sales. The American consumer was more sophisticated than ever before, leading branding to enter a whole new realm, one in which niche marketing—to blacks, gays, women, Hispanics, upscale whites, downscale whites, etc.—became the order of the day.

Today, branding is a more precise field than ever, a melding of science, commerce, and art. And brands themselves have only increased in value, with long-established ones being bought and sold at record prices by companies both here and abroad. Most important of all is that companies of all sizes continue to establish—or at least try to establish—new brands for one simple reason: once a brand is established in the hearts and minds of consumers, it is the most precious marketing commodity of all.

BRANDING AT WORK IN YOUR CAREER

Just as a well-established brand seeps into the public consciousness, so, too, can you brand your identity into the "hearts and minds" of new or prospective bosses, customers, or clients.

By achieving an immediately recognizable identity—your own personal brand—you will become not merely another player in your chosen field, but a power within it.

The goal here is this: to craft an identity that sets you apart on the basis of:

- your unique skills
- needs in the marketplace or in a targeted consumer base
- and the aspects of your personality, where applicable.

When you do this, you are no longer one more among many, but a specialist who can do a job better than anyone else . . . and this holds true whether you are a corporate employee, in private practice, or in the nonprofit sector. In the next chapter, "Making a Name for Yourself," we discuss the principles that will get you on track to achieve just that.

CHAPTER TWO

Making a Name for Yourself

The Career Self-Evaluation and Brand Assessment Tests

So, why do I need to brand myself? Why can't I get ahead simply on the basis of my job performance? The simple answer is this: because if you don't create your own brand, somebody else will create *their* own, and steal the show. Whether it's a corporate job, freelance assignment, or your own business that's your ultimate goal, branding yourself sets you ahead—way ahead—of the pack.

When you have a brand, you become ever so much more than the sum of your parts. No longer merely a competent individual in your chosen field, you are an authority to be reckoned with, and someone other people—be it a corporation or your own company's target market—need.

Imagine, if you will, the typical company's head of personnel. Hundreds, even thousands of résumés pass his or her desk every week. Your mission is clear: to make yours the one chosen, the one that foretells a talent too good to miss. After all, aren't you the wheat and not the chaff?

But if you make the first cut, it's not enough just to show up and have a "good interview." You need a *great* interview, and the way to do that is to brand yourself with a constant and focused eye on the position you want.

But don't believe us. Instead, listen to the words of Carole

Katz, the respected director of recruitment at Warner Brothers, one of the largest entertainment companies in the world. "Establishing a brand and becoming known in your field are key. This has always been true for creative jobs," Katz says, "and now it holds true for people in almost every line of work."

Heath Smith, a longtime executive recruiter for Fortune 500 companies, agrees. "Large companies pay millions of dollars every year to recruit the best people to work for them. People with a branded résumé always end up at the top of the list because their skills and areas of expertise are immediately clear," says Smith.

That's precisely why accountant Jonelle, whom we met in the introduction, has so much more business now than she did last year. By *branding herself* as the accountant who explains the numbers to her clients in plain English, she fulfilled a market need—and now has so many clients she's expanded her practice by hiring another CPA.

Doesn't it stand to reason, then, that we need to brand ourselves no matter which career path we decide to follow? After all, no matter what job we are seeking, the process for finding employment is the same: convincing a new employee or client that we are the right person for the job. "Most résumés are scanned in seconds. If something 'pops' out—like a particular job experience or learned skill— the reader will go back over the résumé for a more thorough review," Smith says. "But unless there is something that catches the reader's eye, your résumé will end up in the 'pass' pile. I don't care whether you're trying to land a corporate job, impress a new client, or are on the job hunt after being downsized out of a job, you need to stand out. You need to provide *something* the résumé reader wants."

In other words, you have to establish a brand. You have to create a name for yourself and, in many cases, you have only seconds to do it. Which is why branding techniques will work for you. Branding techniques were designed to communicate an important message as quickly and effectively as possible.

HOW WELL HAVE YOU BRANDED YOURSELF IN YOUR CAREER? A SELF-EVALUATION.

Before getting started on the brand assessment test, you may want to do a quick pre-evaluation to see where you stand in branding yourself right now. Listed below are fifteen questions to determine how brand-savvy you are about your career. The more honest you are in your answers, the faster you can build your brand. Circle the letter that best describes your situation.

1. The skills I bring to my job are:
   a) Unique and unlike anyone else's in my company or field.
   b) Pretty much like the skills of everyone else who has my job.
   c) Not really the skills needed for my job.
2. How often do you read trade papers or trade magazines to keep up with what is going on in your industry?
   a) At least once a week
   b) At least once a month
   c) Once in a while
   d) Never
3. When was the last time you attended a class to either brush up on your skills or learn new skills for your job?
   a) Within the last six months

b) Six months or longer

c) Never

4. Do you know (circle one):

Your boss's (or clients') favorite color?
Yes or No

Your boss's (or clients') favorite restaurant or food?
Yes or No

Sports or other activities your boss (or clients) like?
Yes or No

5. Do you have a *written* plan of where you want to be in your career three years from now? (circle one)
Yes or No

6. If you were fired tomorrow (or dropped by an important client), do you know your industry well enough to know where you would find your next job? (circle one) Yes or No

7. When was the last time you asked your boss (or client) what skills or abilities were necessary to succeed in your job?

a) Less than six months ago

b) Six months to a year ago

c) Never

8. How important is your personality in successfully carrying out your job?

a) Very important. My personality fits perfectly with my job.

b) Somewhat important. But I could do my job just as well with a different personality.

c) Not important at all. I try to separate my personality from my job.

9. Do you know how valuable you are in the job market? (circle one) Yes or No

10. If you were given a million dollars to do a TV commercial that advertises your most valuable skill,

do you know what the skill would be? (circle one)
Yes or No

11. If you answered yes to question 10, name the skill you would advertise: _____

12. How would you describe the way you feel about your job?
    a) I love my job. My skills and personality fit my job perfectly.
    b) My job is okay. What I'm really good at and what the job requires don't exactly match up.
    c) I'm just passing time until something I really want to do comes along.

13. Do you know what the most important skill your boss (client) is looking for in an employee? (circle one) Yes or No

14. If you answered yes to question 13, name the most important skill your boss (client) is looking for.
    _____

15. Do you know what skills are important in your industry? (circle one) Yes or No

Scoring

Give yourself two points for every "Yes" answer and zero points for every "No" (add up the points and tally the results at the side)   _____

Give yourself two points for every "a" answer, one point for every "b" answer, and zero points for every "c" and "d" answer (add up the points and tally the results at the side)

_____

Give yourself one point each if you answered questions 11 and 14 (add up the points and tally the results at the side)

_____

Bonus: Give yourself three bonus points if the answers to questions 11 and 14 were the same (add up the points and tally the results at the side)   ____

Grand total: please total up the results here   ____

Assessing Your Score: Part One

35 points: Congratulations! You have a strong self-knowledge. You know your brand, understand what your boss (client) expects of you, and have a knowledge of the market and industry in which you compete. You are ready to write your Personal Branding Statement and create your own brand marketing plan, which begins in chapter three.

30 to 34 points: You are well on your way to developing a brand that will set you apart in a very competitive market-place. However, you need to fine-tune a few areas to be truly a star in your field. Go to Assessing Your Score: Part Two to see what areas you should work on to improve career success.

25 to 29 points: You know some important things about yourself and the market in which you compete. But to become a leader in your industry, you need some work. Proceed to Assessing Your Score: Part Two to see what areas to work on.

20 to 24 points: To see success in your chosen field or industry, you're going to need to work on many aspects of your career. To find out where to start, continue to Assessing Your Score: Part Two.

19 points or less: To turn your job into a career, you need to roll up your sleeves and get going. By following the step-by-step process in the following Brand Assessment Test you can

swiftly move to the top of your career. All it takes is sincere desire and hard work.

Assessing Your Score: Part Two

Add up the points from your answers on questions 1, 5, 8, 10, 11, and 12. These questions relate to how well you understand your unique brand. If you scored 9 points or less, you should concentrate on Sections I and II of the Brand Assessment Test. These sections are designed to help you discover the skills, passions, and personality traits that make up your own personal brand.

Add up the points from your answers on questions 4, 7, 13, and 14. These questions relate to how well you know your boss or client, or in brand terms, your target audience. If you scored 9 points or less, Section III of the Brand Assessment Test will help you get to know the most receptive target audience for your brand.

Add up the points from your answers on questions 2, 3, 6, 9, and 15. These questions relate to how much you know about the market and industry in which you compete. If you scored 8 points or less, Section III of the Brand Assessment Test will help you learn more about the market in which you compete.

By working your way through all three sections of the Brand Assessment Test, you will discover your unique brand that will set you apart from your contemporaries, target the boss (client) who will most appreciate your skills and talents, and gain a thorough knowledge of your industry. Before you know it, you'll be ready to create a marketing plan for the most important product out there: you!

MOVING TOWARD CAREER SUCCESS

The formation of a brand is not easy. If it were, every new product would be a raving success and every person in business would be Bill Gates, Donald Trump, or Jill Barad (the president of toy giant Mattel and among the most successful women in corporate business today). It takes research, planning, and a heaping dose of self-awareness to determine your own skill strengths. But it is well worth the effort—especially when you consider that the Coca-Cola brand name alone has been estimated to be worth over $30 billion by *Financial World* magazine.

A well-formulated brand can exponentially increase your net worth, too. Michael Ovitz created a brand for himself as the "superagent of Hollywood." Not only did this successful strategy help him form one of the largest talent agencies in the world, but it eventually landed him a $100 million deal at The Walt Disney Company. You might not see the same quantity of dollar signs in your future, but at the very least, branding yourself should move you up a rung or two on the ladder of riches—and endow you with more respect and recognition from your colleagues or from your competition. That's why we're going to ask you to spend some time to formulate your very own unique brand.

It's worth a little blood, sweat, and tears to create a brand statement that works for you. Put as simply as possible, branding yourself is the single most important thing you can do to establish your worth in the business marketplace—and make you the valuable commodity you deserve to be. And the time to start is *now*. First, though, let's look at how successful consumer products are created, because this process uses the same principles you'll use to research, develop, and establish your own personal brand.

The Process of Creation

New goods or services usually arise for one of two reasons: 1) consumer demand; and 2) technological advancements. But it's important to bear in mind that the creation of a new good or service does not automatically constitute the establishment of a brand; rather, it is merely a new product (with, one hopes, an attendant list of benefits). Which benefits are most significant, how the product fits into the competitive marketplace, how it should be priced, and all other aspects of the marketing mix are still unknown. Not until the experts in the marketing group enter the picture to create a brand statement does a product or service become a brand.

Simply put, the resulting brand statement needs to capture, in a few brief phrases, the essence of the brand, identifying the reasons why the consumer will want to purchase, use, or view the product in preference to its competition. It also needs to "consumerize" the product by stating the technological advancements or updated benefits in a user-friendly way. Case in point: a toothpaste with the active ingredient sodium monofluorophosphate (which serves to negate the buildup of bacteria and plaque) is said by marketers to "fight cavities." Isn't that what we all can understand—and, more important, want?

So, typically, a brand statement includes the following:

• the basic benefits the brand promises to deliver to the consumer
• the product characteristics that make delivery of these promises
• the character or personality of the brand

These three statements thus become the very lifeblood of the brand. From these seemingly simple thoughts derive its pricing, packaging, advertising, promotion, positioning, and distribution. In classic packaged-goods strategy, no decision is made without first consulting this statement, then considering the question: "Is what we are about to do consistent with the brand statement?" If the answer is yes, it is possible to proceed. If it is no, it's time to go back to the drawing board before proceeding. After all, it would be unwise to spend one penny, much less millions of dollars, on an advertising or promotional campaign before feeling confident that the message sent to the consumer underscores the basic statement of the brand.

Stu Fine, vice president of marketing at Alberto-Culver, confirms this view. "I can't stress enough the importance of a strong, concise brand statement. It is the cornerstone of any successful product. Without a winning brand position, a product will drift aimlessly in a highly competitive, highly focused, cutthroat market."

It's easy to know which products have successful brand statements. These brands have a message that tends to stay with you, and when you see or hear the product name you instantly conjure up in your mind what the product does or how it makes you feel. Let's test your brand awareness of some products with successful brand statements:

1. Crest toothpaste:
   a.   tastes great
   b.   fights cavities
   c.   freshens your breath
2. Intel is:
   a.   a chip inside your computer
   b.   a new phone system
   c.   a rock band from Sweden
3. Virginia Slims is:
   a.   the newest diet guru

    b.   a cigarette for women only

    c.   an anorexic character on *Saturday Night Live*

4. Pepsi is:

    a.   made by little elves

    b.   an energy drink

    c.   hipper than Coke

As you probably guessed, the correct answers are: 1, b; 2, a; 3, b; and 4, c.

Whether these brand statements are actually true or not is beside the point, because in the minds of hundreds of millions of people these statements are accepted as the gospel truth. And that is the beauty of a carefully crafted, single-minded, highly focused brand: it presents a premise so carefully devised and so ingrained in our collective psyches that it is accepted as fact. This, in effect, is the point you want to get to with your own brand: who you are and what you can do is accepted by employers or prospective clients not merely as an attractive proposition, but as fact.

FORMING YOUR PERSONAL BRANDING STATEMENT (PBS)

Finding your brand is the cornerstone to a lifetime of career success. It will give you a focal point that will help you make all your career decisions, both small and large. As we stated earlier, in classic packaged goods, no decision is made without first consulting a product's brand statement, and then asking the question: "Is what we are about to do consistent with the brand statement?" Having your own Personal Branding Statement will allow you to do the same, helping you make the correct career choices as you move through life. But how do you go about building your own PBS? That is what we will teach you now. Before plunging headfirst into the Brand Assessment Test (BAT) however, let's look at the approach you'll use as you complete the exercise and discover your brand. It is critical to:

- identify, list, and support your unique skills
- pinpoint your passions and zero in on your prime personality traits
- explore the market to see what skills are most needed, and how your own might best be applied

So, if we were to conjure up a mathematical statement for finding your brand, the following would hold true:

Skills + Personality/Passion + Market Needs =
Your Personal Branding Statement

However, it's not as easy as the equation $2 + 2 = 4$. Building your own branding statement takes devotion and care. As it may well be the single most important effort of your career, you should therefore take the time to accord this project the attention it deserves. We recommend taking thirty to sixty minutes for each of the fifteen sessions to complete the Brand Assessment Test. While some of you may want to rush to finish this assignment, our experience shows that you really do need to do the full fifteen sessions, separated by at least a day per session, to finish the test successfully. Why? Because by giving yourself some breathing room between exercises, you will have time for further reflection—about yourself, your goals, and what you really seek in your professional life.

We hope we convinced you of how important creating your own brand statement is in the first chapter, where we presented individuals from a wide range of fields and showed how they had successfully branded themselves. So let's follow the mathematical brand formula (Skills + Personality/Passion + Market Needs = Your Personal Branding Statement) to determine your unique brand. It may very well change your life—or at the very least, your career.

THE BRAND ASSESSMENT TEST (BAT)

Section I: Uncovering Your Skill Set

In the first section of the BAT we will work on uncovering and understanding your full range of skills. We will prioritize your skills and also come up with very specific examples of when and how you have used each skill. Not only are these exercises designed for self-discovery, but they can be used in the future during job interviews.

We start with working on your skills because, for most people, this will be the basis for forming your brand statement. "Your skill set is usually the first impression a potential employer or client has about you, because it is listed on your résumé," states Heath Smith, executive recruiter. "In many jobs your skills are what you will be 'bringing to the party' and are therefore the most important criteria for employment."

Most products derive the basis for their brand statement from their "skills," or what they do best. For instance, Head and Shoulders shampoo's main "skill" is fighting dandruff. Obviously it has other properties, such as cleaning the hair and making it manageable. But Head and Shoulders' primary attribute, the reason why people purchase it, is its ability to fight dandruff. During the next few sessions, we're going to explore all of your skill sets and determine which are your most powerful.

Session 1: Determining Your Skills

Time required: 60 to 90 minutes
Goal for Session 1: to make a list of your top ten skills and rank them in order of importance

---

All of us have skill sets, those abilities that allow us to complete finite tasks either through natural aptitude and ability; dexterity and coordination; learned knowledge; or any combination of the above. Some skills come naturally to us, while others must be painstakingly learned. However, once they are amassed, the skills you possess—and those you hope to gain—should become a vital part of you and your brand.

In a quiet room, sit down and list (on pages 38–39) what you consider to be your skills. To use a psychological term, "free associate." Don't be afraid to list things that sound stupid, are unrelated to a real job, or anything else that seems irrelevant at first blush. What comes to mind will be not just things you're good at, but things you like to do—and that's the "passion" part of the brand equation.

Nor in this case should you let your conscience be your guide. If you recognize that you are indeed a "good manipulator" of people, put it down: there are more than just a few jobs—in sales, publicity, or as a politician—in which this skill set will lead you to a great on-the-job performance!

As you begin to reflect on your skills, you may find it useful to break them into three main areas:

- *Skills that come naturally to you.* Think back to when you were young, and those things you were good at without having to work too hard, or which you seemed to do better than anyone else. Maybe you had a head for numbers or were mechanically inclined. Perhaps you could play the piano even without reading music, or could sing like Aretha before you were three years old. Think about it some more. Have you always been a natural writer? Do you have the proverbial green thumb? Maybe you were actually the kid chosen for every team at school. Although these things may not, at first glance, seem like they should be part of your branding statement, don't be afraid to write them down. Even something as seemingly superficial as a "trendy dresser" means something: if style is your bag, you might do well to go after jobs in fashion, magazines, or retail, rather than a position with a conservative corporate firm.

• *Skills you acquired through education.* What skills have you gained as a direct result of your educational or vocational training? These may pertain to your current job, but don't limit it to that. Do you speak a foreign language? Are you computer literate? A whiz at repairing small engines? Cook like a dream? Know all of Shakespeare's works, including the sonnets?

• *Skills you acquired on the job.* Beginning with your first job, list all—yes, all—the skills you've acquired. You can prune the list later, but trying to weed it out before you've finished growing it won't serve you well here; just write down your various and sundry skills as they come to you, and think about them later. Go for the general here; getting down to specifics happens later on. For instance, you may wish to include entries like "how to read a formula with metric measurements," "how to do product 'age testing,' " and "knowledge of which chemicals are stable with each other" if you are in product development; or "keeping the weeds at bay and the grass green," "knowing indigenous plants," and "how to bid out and plant a residential garden" if you're a gardening pro. Also consider your personal working style and draw from it. Do you prefer to work alone or do you need the camaraderie of others to get the job done? Is phone work fun, or do you run for the hills whenever you hear the demon ring? Do you prefer to carry on the function of a rigidly defined existing job (if so, the corporate world is for you) or go where no others have dared to go (calling all entrepreneurs)? Consider the parameters of not only your present or most recent job but also the full range of jobs you've held before; this will give you insight to the skills you've held and displayed in a wide range of jobs.

Session 1, Worksheet A: Determining Your Skills

Assignment: List all of your skills from each of the following areas:

Natural Skills:

_____

_____

_____

_____

_____

_____

Skills Acquired through Education:

_____

_____

_____

_____

_____

_____

Skills Acquired on the Job:

_____

_____

_____

_____

Once you have taken an inventory of your skills, look at them again, and circle the ten that you think define what you do best. Then take those ten and list them one at a time in the first column of Session 1, Worksheet B on page 40.

Now, remember what we said earlier about taking a product's benefits and making them *consumer-friendly?* For example, a toothpaste's technical ability to create stronger tooth enamel and prevent plaque translates to the much more approachable—and memorable—"fights cavities." As the next assignment within Session 1, take each of the skills from your "top ten list" and turn it into a benefit to your "consumer"—that is, your prospective boss if you're looking for a staff job, or your clients, if you run or are planning to start your own business or practice. Case in point: if one of your skills is "meeting deadlines," you can "consumerize" it into a meaningful benefit by saying something like "100 percent track record of never being late with a report or assignment." This becomes an especially attractive trait to a prospective boss in any industry where deadlines are famously tight. Here are a few more examples:

Skill: Instinctively understand how engines and other mechanical devices function
Consumerized: I've never seen a problem with a car engine that I couldn't fix

Skill: Conceptual thinker
Consumerized: Love to take ideas and turn them into business realities

Skill: Know how to use all search engines on the Internet
Consumerized: Expert Web surfer who can get you information fast and efficiently

Look at your list again, then number your skills from best to worst, using 1 for the best and 10 for the worst. This in no way means that you'll end up doing, or even pursuing, your top skill, but it gives you an idea of what you think you do best, and/or which skill is or might become more important to you. For example, if you're a doctor, your top skill might be "highly effective emergency room treatment." Even if you're thinking of changing specialties by going into research or private practice, the fact that you consider ER your top skill may have you thinking twice about what you should be doing. Or it may not. But it will have you thinking cogently about what your ultimate brand should be.

Session 1, Worksheet B: Consumerizing Your Ten Best Skills

My Top Ten Skills	My Top Ten Skills Consumerized
1.	1.
2.	2.
3.	3.
4.	4.
5.	5.
6.	6.
7.	7.
8.	8.
9.	9.
10.	10.

Session 2: Proof of Claims for Each Skill

Recommended time: 60 minutes
**Goal: to provide as many examples as possible for your top
ten skills as proof to substantiate each one**

In Session 1 you amassed your top-ten skill list; now let's
put your skills to the test. At this point your job is to prove
each skill with *concrete examples*. Approach this with a
totally positive and open mind, because this isn't work—it's
laying the foundation for wowing a prospective boss or customer by bringing to the surface and highlighting skills you
use better than anyone else. As such, this exercise represents
a giant first step toward finding your brilliant brand.

Why is the proof necessary? Say that you listed "self-
starter" as one of your skills. Terrific! Problem is, without
providing a factual backdrop, this sounds like a cliché, and a
vapid one at that. It's like those bad résumés that state "self-
starter, cheerful and optimistic, a team player." Well, aren't
we all? Who's ever seen the obverse, "slothful, downtrodden
loner," on a résumé? Also, in an interview, it is imperative to
have concrete, well-thought-out examples of your skills that
you can quickly reel off to the interviewer. By working on
these answers now, they can become second nature to you
during the job hunt. So, show, don't tell. For each skill, list
several supporting truths. For instance:

Skill: Creates and executes projects without being asked
or requiring anyone's help
Consumerized: Independent self-starter
Proof:
• When I needed funding for a research project and the
school wouldn't help with funding, I set out to find an alternative funding source and ended up finding three.

• I contacted the governing board of an international educational conference with an idea for a new seminar series, which is now part of the annual conference.

• When my department couldn't afford to send me to a national conference, I independently submitted and later presented a paper to the conference board. The board was so impressed, they paid my way to the conference.

One of our clients just completed this worksheet. He came up with the following list:

Top Ten Skills	Top Ten Skills Consumerized	Proof of Claims of Top Ten Skills
1. Excellent verbal communication	1. Can speak to any-one about anything	• Runner-up, Toastmasters National Competition • Rated top sales-person three years in a row for oral presentations
2. Can handle large volumes of work	2. Hard worker with demonstrable skills	• Ran two sales units (usually manned by two people) with an increase in sales in both units
3. Highly organized	3. Highly organized	• Reputation for having the neatest desk and files • Took the Franklin Covey course in organization

Top Ten Skills	Top Ten Skills Consumerized	Proof of Claims of Top Ten Skills
4. Driven to succeed	4. Highly motivated	• First-string college football • Worked full-time while going to college
5. Congenial with coworkers	5. Works well with everyone	• Always selected for group projects • Known as team player
6. Excellent understanding of math	6. Good head for numbers	• Scored in top tenth percentile on GMAT math section
7. High level of energy	7. Energetic	• Everyone says I have more energy than anyone else
8. Fluent in Japanese	8. Speaks Japanese	• Lived in Japan for two years as only foreigner in small city
9. Physically fit	9. In good shape	• Yearly checkups confirm healthy mind and body • Work out at gym 4x/week
10. Computer literate	10. Good with computers	• Know all Microsoft business software • Owned computer for over ten years

Now complete this activity using each of your ten top skills you listed on your Session 1, Worksheet B.

Session 2 Worksheet

Assignment: Write down your top ten skills, then consumerize them to make them meaningful to your boss (or client), and then give at least two examples that provide the best proof of each skill.

Top Ten Skills	Top Ten Skills Consumerized	Proof of Claims of Top Ten Skills
1.	1.	• •
2.	2.	• •
3.	3.	• •
4.	4.	• •
5.	5.	• •
6.	6.	• •

Top Ten Skills	Top Ten Skills Consumerized	Proof of Claims of Top Ten Skills
7.	7.	• •
8.	8.	• •
9.	9.	• •
10.	10.	• •

Once you've completed the worksheet, consider the following question: Is each skill cogently supported by my proofs? If the answer is yes, superb. If it's no, you need to think some more about specific proof you can provide for your skills. You may want to set the worksheet aside for a while and return to it when you have thought of some stronger proofs while shopping, in the bathroom, or at the gym.

If you're absolutely unable to come up with supporting proofs for your skill statements, these probably aren't skills you should place in your top ten. You may indeed strive toward these in the future—as the most successful of all self-branders do—but you shouldn't plan on using these to your advantage if these "skills" exist only in your mind. If you listed "self-starter" among your skills, but the only proof you could come up with is having changed the toilet paper in the bathroom at your workplace, that's not self-starting—it's necessity, and the two are very different skills indeed!

Session 3: One-on-One Focus Groups: Part One

Recommended time: 30 minutes
Goal: to get outside agreement that the skills and proofs you selected best reflect your skill sets

---

In product branding, as carried out by America's largest and most sophisticated companies, consumer research is an ongoing business tool. Within the many research methods used, focus groups are top priority. Indeed, they represent the gates through which all new products or line extensions must pass. Focus groups comprise a random sample of about ten people—typically consumers of the brand—to talk about the product or service as it is and as they'd like it to be. Most of the time, a series of groups are held, though one-on-one surveys (where one researcher talks to one consumer at a time) are also standard. One-on-ones are conducted so that consumers are not influenced by groupthink. In well-conducted focus group explorations, the marketer exits with a strong idea of what consumers like and dislike about a product, as well as what they think it does and wish it would do. Inevitably, the brand marketer is graced with a fresh, new perspective on the product, one emanating directly from consumers (who may have very different ideas from those of the corporate types who think up new products!).

That said, you are now going to conduct your own version of a focus group as a means of ascertaining that your skill set and proofs do indeed match up. Select five people who know you, whether in business or as a friend. We always advise choosing from among colleagues and companions alike for a broad-based, general view.

Using the one-on-one format, show each chosen member of your focus group your set of skills and proof of claims from your Session 2 worksheet. Give it to them in person, fax it, or even e-mail it; waste no time with "snail mail"! Ask them for their opinion, however brutal this may be. Let them know this is not a validation of your strength of character or goodness of person, merely a list of your professional strengths, so they shouldn't back off from the truth. And you then need to make sure that you respond with an open mind and heart to their perception. Go ahead and do it now.

So . . . do your focus group members agree with both your skills and the proofs provided? Are they of the same mind regarding your order of relative skill strengths? Most important of all, are there other skills they would attribute to you that you yourself have missed? There's a reason we've asked you to choose your focus groups from people you know well and not merely from disinterested parties: whether these folks are old friends or business acquaintances, they may well see strengths (and, yes, weaknesses) you were unaware of. By going through this process, which may be painful at times, you will arrive at the other end with a thorough knowledge of what your strengths—and weaknesses—are, and you will be in a much better position to follow the career path of your dreams.

Session 4: Reevaluation

Recommended time: 30 minutes
Goal: to review the work done in Sessions 1–3, make any changes necessary, and recap what you have learned about yourself through working through these sessions

Having shared your thoughts with the outside world, now is the time to rethink and regroup. First, consider each person's comments. Do you agree with them? If so, incorporate their thoughts and suggestions in your skills/proof of claims document (pages 44–45). Are there new skills to add? Any skills to remove? Should the skill order be changed? Remember, your Personal Branding Statement is still a work in progress, and you shouldn't be afraid to switch things around or rethink them at this point. Even when your branding statement is completed, it isn't set in stone.

Once you have incorporated the results of your one-on-one focus groups into your own document, carefully review the work that you have done and pat yourself on the back. This work isn't easy, but the rewards are great.

Now take a few minutes and write down on your Session 4 worksheet everything you have learned so far about yourself, your skills, where you want to go in your career, and how perceptions about yourself and your career have changed by working through these sessions. When you're finished it'll be time to start Section II.

Session 4 Worksheet

Assignment: Write down everything you have learned so far about yourself, your skills, where you want to go in your career, and how perceptions about yourself, your skills, and your career have changed.

_____

_____

_____

_____

_____

_____

_____

_____

_____

_____

_____

_____

Section II: Uncovering Your Passion/Defining Your Personality

In the first section of the BAT, we looked at your skill sets and backed them up with proofs, providing an objective evaluation of what you do best. Here we consider the more subjective elements of your personality and passions—brand components that are every bit as important as your skill set statement. Because, all other things being equal, many companies select employees based on their personality, style, and other outward factors, it is especially important that you are aware of these external elements of your brand. In fact, there are some careers, such as that of a flight attendant or model, where personality and appearance are paramount, and those skill sets are taught in training school or on the job. Headhunter Karen Rosenthal echoes this sentiment. "Particular personalities just seem to work better in certain businesses," she believes. "Obviously a potential job candidate must be competent and technically proficient, but then I look at their personality and demeanor. I always interview someone over dinner so they can be relaxed and their true personality can emerge."

Of course, brands, too, are often sold on their personality as opposed to their benefits. These are known to marketers as image brands; their personas don't convey one overwhelming product benefit, but rather conjure up an emotion or image. These brands try to "romance" the consumer into using them. Swatch watches and any fragrance are strong examples of image brands; so are the tourist campaigns of Israel, Spain, or any other country that advertises. And if Joe Camel wasn't perceived as a cool dude, why were cigarette manufacturers so upset when concerned parents fought to get the character out of magazines and off billboards across the U.S.A.?

Coke and Pepsi are two of the world's most recognizable image-based brands. Each has a distinct personality, yet neither refers to the product's benefits or even its taste. Rather, Coke is "the real thing" and Pepsi is "for generation Next." Neither positioning has anything to do with the products' attributes per se, but with their perceived personalities.

If these products were sold exclusively on their benefits (in the human paradigm, their skill sets) consumers would be looking for such things as taste, color, packaging, carbonation level, and caffeine content. Yet none of these things is ever mentioned in ads for Pepsi or Coke. Instead, it is their personalities that drive these brands.

Depending on your professional aspirations, your brand may also be personality driven; and, at the very least, this is a component of virtually every profession, even those you'd probably think immune—Like book publishing, for example. Literary agent, Katharine Sands is a genius at matching books with editors because, unlike some agents who force every proposal on every editor they've ever met, Katharine totally understands editors' brands. In fact, editors brand themselves by their office decor and wardrobe to announce "serious fiction editor," "pop culture enthusiast," and everything in between.

High-technology companies also have a very distinct personality. Microsoft, for example, has a fairly informal dress policy that allows sweaters instead of suit coats and ties for the men and pants instead of dresses for women. This "personality trait" helps breaks down barriers for better interaction between different divisions and layers of management.

So now let's focus on finding your personality and passion in this part of the Brand Assessment Test.

Session 5: What's Your Passion?

Recommended time: 30 to 60 minutes
Goal: to discover what your passions are

Below and on the following page, write a paragraph or two, or merely bullet points, on the following subject: "If I didn't have to work, here's what I would do all day long."

We've all thought about this, of course; now is your chance to put those daydreams into writing. How would you spend your sixteen waking hours if you didn't have to go to work or open a store? And "have fun" is not a valid answer; we're looking for specifics: Where would you go? What precisely would you do? Without thinking of whether they're right or wrong, intellectual or vacuous, legal or not, write them all down, as many or as few as you'd like.

A lucky few, bless your hearts, will write down exactly what you happen to be doing already, or some slight variation thereof—and that, of course, is the point we'd all like to get to. But for now, all we ask is thirty to sixty minutes during which you fully consider what you like to do best of all. Have fun with this assignment!

Session 5 Worksheet

Assignment: In writing, answer the following question: "If I didn't have to work, here's what I would do all day long."

_____
_____
_____
_____
_____
_____
_____

_____

_____

_____

_____

_____

Session 6: Personality Traits

Recommended time: 30 minutes
Goal: to determine your ten most powerful personality traits

We have compiled a list of eighty adjectives used to describe standard personality traits. Take a minute to look this list over, then put a check by all those traits that best describe you.

Active	Dependable	Healthy
Adaptable	Diplomatic	Helpful
Aggressive	Dramatic	Humorous
Aloof	Driven	Imaginative
Ambitious	Dynamic	Insensitive
Argumentative	Easygoing	Intelligent
Assertive	Emotional	Introverted
Calm	Empowering	Impatient
Candid	Encouraging	Inventive
Careless	Enterprising	Leaderlike
Cheerful	Entertaining	Likable
Colorful	Enthusiastic	Materialistic
Competitive	Ethical	Methodical
Confident	Experienced	Moody
Conservative	Extroverted	Open-minded
Convincing	Flexible	Optimistic
Cooperative	Forceful	Orderly
Creative	Forward-thinking	Organized
Credible	Friendly	Original
Daring	Headstrong	Patient

Persuasive	Savvy	Tolerant
Procrastinating	Self-centered	Trusting
Productive	Sensitive	Visionary
Resilient	Shy	Well adjusted
Resourceful	Stubborn	Well connected
Restless	Supportive	Witty
Risk-taking	Temperamental	

Now comes the hard part. Narrow the list down to ten characteristics that most accurately describe your personality profile. Then: Are there any adjectives not on the list that better reflect who you are? Fine. Substitute whichever ones you'd like to complete your personality trait list. Please complete the worksheet for Session 6 even if you, like us, hate this kind of exercise. There's a very valid reason we ask you to do so, one you may have already guessed: we'll ask you to use this character portrait to perfect your final brand. It's a reality check of sorts, especially for clients who list "aggressive," "materialistic," and "self-centered," then tell us they want to head up a nonprofit organization.

Session 6 Worksheet

Assignment: to write down the ten personality traits that best describe you.

1. _____
2. _____
3. _____
4. _____
5. _____
6. _____
7. _____
8. _____
9. _____
10. _____

Session 7: Scaling

Recommended time: 30 minutes
Goal: to determine the intensity or strength of certain personality traits

---

In this session we will continue our work on personality traits. We have created a list of word opposites, with the numbers 1 through 8 in between each word. Look at both words on each line and determine which of the two words best describes your personality. Then, using the number scale between the words, figure out where your personality best fits and circle that number. For example, in looking at the antonyms "driven" and "apathetic," if you feel "driven" most closely, but not completely, describes your personality, you might circle the number 2 or 3. However, if you feel "driven" completely describes a personality trait of yours, you would circle the number 1. This is called "scaling," and is used to determine the intensity or strength of certain traits. For the first part of this session, complete the scaling worksheet below and on page 55.

Session 7 Worksheet

Assignment: On a scale of 1 to 8, rate yourself on where your personality falls within each set of words. The closer the numbers are to the word, the closer your personality fits with the word.

Active	1	2	3	4	5	6	7	8	Passive
Adaptable	1	2	3	4	5	6	7	8	Inflexible
Aloof	1	2	3	4	5	6	7	8	Friendly
Athletic	1	2	3	4	5	6	7	8	Inactive
Candid	1	2	3	4	5	6	7	8	Evasive
Cheerful	1	2	3	4	5	6	7	8	Grumpy

Competitive	1	2	3	4	5	6	7	8	Nonaggressive
Conservative	1	2	3	4	5	6	7	8	Liberal
Dishonest	1	2	3	4	5	6	7	8	Trustworthy
Depressed	1	2	3	4	5	6	7	8	Happy
Driven	1	2	3	4	5	6	7	8	Apathetic
Easygoing	1	2	3	4	5	6	7	8	Uptight
Effective	1	2	3	4	5	6	7	8	Ineffective
Eloquent	1	2	3	4	5	6	7	8	Tongue-tied
Enthusiastic	1	2	3	4	5	6	7	8	Blasé
Farsighted	1	2	3	4	5	6	7	8	Shortsighted
Insensitive	1	2	3	4	5	6	7	8	Sensitive
Introverted	1	2	3	4	5	6	7	8	Extroverted
Irresponsible	1	2	3	4	5	6	7	8	Responsible
Likable	1	2	3	4	5	6	7	8	Unlikable
Moody	1	2	3	4	5	6	7	8	Serene
Optimistic	1	2	3	4	5	6	7	8	Pessimistic
Organized	1	2	3	4	5	6	7	8	Scattered
Late	1	2	3	4	5	6	7	8	Timely
Solitary	1	2	3	4	5	6	7	8	Sociable
Trusting	1	2	3	4	5	6	7	8	Skeptical
Reckless	1	2	3	4	5	6	7	8	Prudent
Witty	1	2	3	4	5	6	7	8	Humorless

Once you have completed the worksheet, circle those traits for which you rated yourself either a 1 or an 8. Now go back to the Session 6 worksheet where you listed your top ten personality traits. Are there any traits on that list that are the same as the words you just rated yourself as either a 1 or an 8? If so, keep note of this to use it when we begin to build your Personal Branding Statement.

Session 8: One-on-One Focus Groups: Part Two

Recommended time: 30 minutes
Goal: to get outside agreement that the personality traits you selected best reflect your true personality

As you did with your skill set focus groups in Session 3, target five people and show them your work in this section. You can use the same people or different ones, depending on their availability and your choice. Show each of the focus test members:

- your paragraph(s) on your passions
- the ten adjectives that best describe your personality
- the words from the scaling exercise that you rated yourself either a 1 or an 8

Again ask for complete honesty. Do they agree with your conclusions? Are there other adjectives they would use for your personality? If so, do you agree with them? (If three or more people mention the same adjective, even if you don't agree, perhaps you should consider this as a trait you didn't realize you had.) Once you have conducted your one-on-one research, meld their reactions with the self-branding data you have formed in this section to form a new, synergistic profile of your personality and passions.

Session 9: Reevaluation

Recommended time: 30 minutes
Goal: to review the work done in Sessions 5–8, make any changes necessary, and recap what you have learned about yourself through working through these sessions

---

You have amassed a cohesive set of data—that's terrific! As we've said before, this isn't easy work, but the dividends are unending. During this session reflect back on all the work from Sessions 5 through 7. After the one-on-ones you conducted in Session 8, is all the information still accurate? If not, make any changes you wish to now. You should have the following worksheets complete:

- a roster of your passions
- a list of ten adjectives that best describe your personality
- a completed scaling exercise pinpointing many of your strong characteristics

Now carefully review the work that you have done. Congratulate yourself. Few people know as much about themselves as you are learning.

To wind up this section, take a few minutes and write down on your Session 9 worksheet everything you have learned in this section about yourself, your personality, and your passions, and how your passions and personality fit into your career path. Or if they don't fit in, how can you make them fit? How has your perception about yourself and your career changed by working through these sessions? After you finish this session, you're ready to tackle Section III.

Session 9 Worksheet

Assignment: Write down everything you have learned so far about yourself, your passions and personality, where you want to go in your career, and how perceptions about yourself and your career have changed.

_____

_____

_____

_____

_____

_____

_____

_____

_____

_____

_____

_____

Section III: Exploring the Marketplace

In the past two sections, we have identified your skill set, passions, and personality. These areas form two-thirds of your brand equation. But without the next piece of the puzzle, your brand is incomplete. It is now time to look beyond your skills, personality, and passion to the marketplace and its competitive environment. For it is here where you will be taking your skills and competing with everyone else in your field.

Before proceeding, however, be certain that you have a definite picture of the field you are pursuing; without this as a target, a survey of the market is premature. If you are in the process of changing careers or selecting an initial one, don't despair. Do what we advise our own clients: pick one of the fields or job categories you are interested in, and start there. Not only will this allow you to complete Section III, but it may also help you finalize your decision about which field or job area you want to pursue. If, after going through the next session, you decide the field you researched isn't one you want to go into, no problem; you can retake this section any time with a new industry or job in mind.

So let's proceed to find the last element of your campaign: how you stack up versus the competition, and how to define an unoccupied market niche for your brand.

> ### Session 10: Your Chosen Field and Job
>
> **Recommended time: 30 to 45 minutes**
> **Goal: to thoroughly understand the job responsibilities, skills, and personality required for your current job**

As career consultants, we are constantly astounded by one fact above all others about our clients: There is not a lack of skills nor a lack of caring but, amazingly, a lack of knowledge of the options available in their own fields, much less those of allied or new ones.

Even more shocking is many clients' inability to cite and document the duties, responsibilities, and achievements of their *present* jobs in the strongest possible terms. Which is precisely why we spend so much time rethinking and rewriting résumés.

In order to brand yourself well, you need to first understand the function of your present position or business, then deduce what you bring to the table more effectively than anyone else. Thus in this session we are going to ask that you do the following on the Session 10 worksheet:

1. Write down the title of your current position or type of business you are currently in.
2. List:
    a) the general responsibilities of this post
    b) the specific duties required
    c) any achievements you have made
3. List the key talents and skills you believe are necessary to succeed in your present post.

Here's how a client filled out her worksheet:
Present position: Secretary

Job responsibilities: Oversee the administrative duties for the vice president of sales

Specific duties: Answer phones, set schedules, type memos, fill out expense reports, handle weekly sales reports from the five district managers, make all arrangements for sales conferences

Achievements: Created new system for sales reports; designed new filing system; set forth proposal of how to set up new sales offices district by district

Key talents and skills necessary: Organizational skills to manage heavy phone traffic as well as meeting constant requests from boss; patience to handle a huge amount of questions and the constant rearranging of hotel and plane reservations; high level of computer skills including knowledge of Microsoft Word, Excel, and Memomate; and ability to maintain cool under intense pressure when the phones are ringing, the boss is screaming, and the weekly report needs to get out.

Now it's your turn. Note: If you are a recent graduate looking for your first job you can work on this session in one of two ways: either fill in each of the areas based on your fantasy job position (how you think the perfect job would be) or base your answers on a job that you have had in the past. If you are between jobs now, fill out the worksheet based on your most recent position.

Session 10 Worksheet

Assignment: To understand the complete job responsibility, duties, and skills required for your current job and your achievements in this job.

Present position: _____

Job responsibilities:

_____

_____

Specific duties:

Achievements:

Key talents and skills:

Session 11: Your Chosen Field and Job—continued

Recommended time: 2 to 4 hours now, and with open eyes for the rest of your working life
Goal: to become an expert and authority in and about your chosen field

---

The aim of this exercise is to continue to expand your knowledge of your specific field and general professional area through research and information seeking. It may seem overly academic at first, but if you're like the overwhelming majority of our clients, you'll soon become a research junkie for one simple reason: you are certain to find new opportunities within your field that you never knew existed, and which you'll be gung ho to explore. Many of our clients come to us feeling boxed in, as if they had no options, but the reality is quite the contrary. In fact, typically this exercise has one very happy ending: you'll feel like the world is your oyster.

To begin, start boning up on the organizations in your field—and virtually every trade or profession has at least one. If you're a doctor, contact the American Medical Association. A hairstylist? Call the Beauty Council of America. A writer? Get in touch with the National Association of Journalists or the Author's Guild.

You say you don't know where to look for the leading organizations in your field? Then we'll tell you: Get ye to the Internet! Yahoo, Excite, Lycos, and other leading search engines allow you to type in a key word or phrase about the field or job in which you have an interest (e.g., attorney, salesman, bank officer, police officer, ventriloquist) and you're almost sure to find key associations governing that field. If you don't find sufficient data from the Web (which would be hard to believe), proceed to the nearest library to look for the Encyclopedia of Associations. In fact, go to the library regardless of whether you find sources on the Web or not, because uncovering every stone is vital. Why stop at contacting two organizations when you might find ten?

Once you have uncovered all the organizations in your field, contact them by phone, fax, letter, or e-mail, and ask that they send you any and all information they might have. A press kit is de rigueur; brochures, mission statements, and other materials should also be available. These documents will tell you if the field is growing or shrinking, where the jobs are, new skills required, pay levels, geographical constraints and/or opportunities, what the future holds, and other important trends in your general area.

Knowledge is power, and it could hardly be truer than in this case. Most people have no firm game plan for their careers. A major part of branding yourself, on the other hand, is knowing who you are and where the opportunities lie. Don't just ride in the back of the truck; pave your own road to success by knowing exactly where you want to go!

If you are currently in a job with a mid- to large-size company, you should have in hand your job description. If not, call the human resource department to ask for a copy of this document. Many smaller companies don't have a formal document, but check with your supervisor to see if he or she has a job description. If not, you may want to ask to see the ad they use when recruiting for the job, or offer to write up a job description based on your experience.

When you have all the information gathered, from the very broad industry information to the very narrow job description of your job, compare it with what you had written down about your job on the Session 10 worksheet. How closely does the data align? If there are discrepancies, you need to decide if your own expectations and concept of your job are higher or lower than those of the outside resources whose data you've amassed. It might be time to reevaluate how you feel about your job; or, on a more positive note, this research and reflection may well provide the beginning of a unique brand that truly sets you apart from the field.

If you have just graduated and are looking for your first job, or are currently between jobs, try to get a description of the job you have your eye on. You may be able to obtain this through your school's employment center, through the company's Web site, or perhaps through a friend who currently has the job, or one similar to, the one you are interested in. Once you have the job description, compare it to your Session 10 worksheet to see areas of similarity and areas that don't match up. Were your expectations in line with reality or were they off the mark? Are the skills you cited on the Session 10 worksheet the same as those needed for the new job?

If not, how different are they? After comparing notes, you may want to reevaluate the direction you are headed or continue full speed ahead knowing expectations and reality are in check.

Session 12: Determining Your Target Audience

Recommended time: 60 minutes
Goal: to understand who you should be targeting with your unique skills set and personality

---

Let your mind flow freely now, and if you're in the corporate world, describe your perfect boss. Or if you work independently or have your own practice or business, who is your ideal audience or customer? You may develop the best brand statement in the world, but it's all for naught if you don't get the message out to the right targets. Your target audience will differ depending on where you currently are in your career, and what you want to do.

If you're in the corporate world your primary target audience will be your direct boss. If you're a consultant, are self-employed, or have your own business, you need to figure out who your customer base will be—specifically. By understanding who you're targeting—that is, to whom you want your brand to most appeal—you'll gain insight into your overall brand character.

When deciding on your target audience, you will look at many factors. Two of the most common factors are demographics and psychographics—that is, an audience's lifestyle and affinities. Under demographics, you may want to consider:

- age: young, middle-aged, or elderly
- geographical location: neighborhood, city, state, national, or international

- job status: white-collar, working class, retired
- income: low, middle, high
- gender: male or female
- education: high school, college, postgraduate

Under psychographics you may want to consider:

- lifestyle: family, single, gay, or straight
- politics: conservative or liberal
- philosophy on money: thrifty and responsible or big spender
- mind-set: innovator or follower, artistic or business-oriented, loves parties or is a homebody

These questions are basically the same whether you're opening a restaurant, a clothing store, a medical office, or a bank. Who do you seek to target with your brilliant new brand?

Now, if you're on staff at a company or organization of any size, your target search is different but should be carried out with no less a concerted effort. In fact, as career consultants, we're here to tell you that a lack of clear targeting—for new jobs, career changes, or promotions—is one of the main reasons people don't get the positions they want. And yet, since this is one of the easiest factors to control, there's no excuse for shooting yourself in the foot because of a poorly planned target list.

As mentioned before, your ultimate target audience in a corporate job will be your immediate boss. However, you may have to target other people in other areas of the company to get the job. Many people sabotage their job campaigns by failing to know exactly to whom they should be pitching, or where they should be networking. In some companies, for instance, human resource people are mere paper pushers (in which case you should be contacting the head of the department—accounting, legal, finance, marketing, sales, etc., in which you want to work). At other firms they are solid professionals, and the gatekeepers through whom even the most senior management must pass. To the fullest extent possible, get to know who does what at the key companies you've been targeting for your campaign.

But that's not enough. It's important to know if the firm is hip or conservative, progressive or staid, so you know how to come across when the interview time comes. Ought you to be fashion forward or Brooks Brothers–clad; gung ho or reserved? How does the company communicate: by phone, fax, e-mail, or in person? The more you know about your target, down to the little details, the more successful you will be. One client shared with us that it wasn't until she discovered that her target audience liked their memos typed in Bookman font that she finally made headway with them!

The following is a target audience composite of who the perfect target audience would be for one of our clients who runs her own public relations firm and specializes in providing services for high-end luxury goods companies. Much of her success is her incredible understanding of who her target audience is. Keep in mind that this isn't a profile of any one person; rather, it is a composite of her ideal target audience:

The target audience for the Julia Van Hees brand is a male in his mid 40s to 50s. He has a true sense of sophistication and unique flair. He stands out in a crowd not because he is the most handsome, but because of his charisma and how he presents himself. He works out and knows how to care for his health. He probably owns his own company, and very likely built it from the ground up.

He never ceases to develop interests. Outside of his career, he maintains an active—almost too busy—social life. He enjoys the theater and arts. He is inspired by the social panorama of the city in which he lives, and attends galas and openings as a means of cultivating ideas and staying in touch with both popular culture and high arts. He is friendly with those both in high and low places, and is almost universally admired for his character and kindness.

My target audience is fashion oriented, yet not a slave to fashion. He knows what works for him and what doesn't. He is very selective in adding to his wardrobe, and knows how to combine high-end lines with more moderately priced clothing.

He treats employees like friends, for he knows that treating people well produces better work and a sense of long-term loyalty.

This profile covers both the demographic and psychographic aspects of our client's target audience. The detail is so vibrant, you could pick out this person in a crowd (if he were real rather than a composite). This detailed knowledge of who your target audience is will be critical to your success whether you're an entrepreneur or a corporate employee. Knowing your target audience, what his/her dislikes and likes are, what he/she expects from you (and knowing what you can and can't deliver) makes your job of succeeding that much easier.

Using the above as a guide, write a similar synopsis of whom you would like to work for and/or who would be your ideal customer.

Session 12 Worksheet

Assignment: Describe in detail who your perfect boss or target customer would be.

_____

_____

_____

_____

_____

_____

_____

_____

_____

_____

_____

_____

Session 13: Thinking Like the Customer

Recommended time: 60 minutes
Goal: to understand what is important to our target audience

Before we can look for a job, find new customers, or pitch ourselves for a promotion, we need to know exactly who we are and what we are offering, and be aware of not just our own needs but those of our target audience(s). This is a tactic every smart self-brander has down pat.

Thus, your goal for this session is to put yourself in your target audience's shoes and first think about and then answer two questions: 1) If you were your target audience—your boss, customer, or client—what would he or she think are the most important aspects of your job, either your current job or business or, if you are currently searching for a job, the job you would like to have?; and 2) How does that perspective compare to how *you* view the job?

Remember, your frame of reference is no longer just you, but the person or audience who will receive your brand messages as well. If you are currently employed, your frame of reference should be your boss or clients. If you have just graduated from school, are currently unemployed, or employed and looking for a new job or trying to bring in new clients, use as your frame of reference the audience you are planning on targeting. If you don't know who your target audience is just yet, use as your frame of reference the ideal target audience you wrote about in Session 12.

Some of the things you may want to consider writing about are the following: What is missing from the job? Should any responsibilities or areas of authority be added or taken away? Are there areas that are ignored and, conversely, is too much time being spent on certain tasks? Also think about your target audience's priorities.

As an example, let's see how Mike, a national sales manager for a large consumer goods company, worked on this exercise.

Target Audience: Buyers at all the accounts I call on. Altogether, there are twenty main buyers.

What's Important to Me	What's Important to My Target Audience (Account Buyers)
• Sell each account as much product as possible	• Buy minimum quantities to keep shelves stocked
• Spend as little money as possible at each account	• Get as much money as possible to spend on in-store advertising and promotion, etc.
• Maintain a good relationship with all my buyers	• Don't care about relationship with salesman
• Meet with buyers as often as possible	• Meet only when necessary
• Be on time for all scheduled appointments	• Be on time for all scheduled appointments

What's Important to Me	What's Important to My Target Audience (Account Buyers)
• Give a well-thought-out presentation	• Have a well-thought-out presentation
• Make sure the products sell through	• Make sure the products sell through

As you can see, there are significant differences between what is important to Mike and what's important to his target audience. But there are also areas that are important to both Mike and his target audience.

Areas of importance to both Mike and his target audience: being on time for scheduled appointments, have a well-thought-out presentation, and making sure product sells through.

Areas of importance to Mike only: selling as much product as possible, spending as little money as possible, meeting as often as possible, and building a good relationship with buyer.

Areas of importance to the target audience only: buy minimum product, get as much advertising money as possible, meet only when necessary, don't build a relationship with salesman.

If, after evaluation, you find out what is important to you and what is important to your customer/audience is completely different, you may decide that this job or association isn't the right target for you. You may decide that what you bring to the party may not be a good fit when it comes to how they evaluate your job. As painful as it can sometimes be, it is better to know up front rather than to waste valuable time and resources on a target that won't be productive. If you do come to this decision, you must start the process of selecting a target audience over and over again until you find some areas where you overlap and your goals are consistent.

Now it's your turn.

Session 13 Worksheet

Assignment: Specify your target audience, then answer two questions: 1) If you were your target audience—your boss, customer, or client—what would he or she think are the most important aspects of your job, either your current job or business or, if you are currently searching for a job, the job you would like to have?; and 2) How does that perspective compare to how you view the job?

Target Audience: _____

What's Important to Me	What's Important to My Target Audience
•	•
•	•
•	•
•	•
•	•
•	•
•	•

Areas that are important to me and my target audience: _____
_____

Areas that are important to me and not my target audience: _____
_____

Areas that are important to my target audience and not me:

_____

_____

Session 14: One-on-One Focus Groups: Part Three

Recommended time: 30 minutes
Goal: to get outside agreement that the work done on building industry knowledge and defining the target audience is correct

---

In this session you will once again review and examine outside opinions on your attitudes toward your job, business, or targeted field. Select five people to participate. Unlike the other one-on-one focus groups you have gathered, these people should preferably be in your field or chosen fields and understand the nature of your current job or job you aspire to. In other words, they should have enough of a clue to make informed judgments on the specific information you are about to present. If you have been doing research on a field that is new to you and you don't know many people in the field, we recommend the Internet as a resource to find people in your new field. We've actually conducted this portion of our one-on-one focus groups on-line and via e-mail!

On an individual basis, share the results of exercises from days ten to thirteen with them. Ask for their candid points of view regarding the analyses you've already made: Are the conclusions accurate? Do they have any other suggestions? What might be missing from either the small or big picture? Because these people have at least some knowledge of your field of expertise, yet aren't as close to your brand-in-progress as you are, they're apt to come up with points of difference you haven't seen.

Session 15: Reevaluation

Recommended time: 60 minutes
Goal: to review the work done in the past fourteen sessions and make final changes before creating your Personal Branding Statement

---

This is the last work session of the Brand Assessment Test. You should review the results of the past five sessions, then synthesize these findings with the rest of your work from Sessions 1–9. Among the issues to consider:

• What are the gaps between what you perceive your current or desired job, business, or service to be and what your boss or customer would like it to be?

• Do these gaps provide a window of opportunity or niche to do something different? If so, what? Don't stop at just one thought here—probe and explore. Nor should you fail to list options because you think they're too hard, too expensive, or too weird; let your mind go free, then come back to reality later on as you make your final analysis and review.

• Are there gaps between what is presently done on the job or how a business is run and what you think should ideally be the case? These gaps are often valid market niches, holes in the marketplace that you can fill with your brand to experience stellar success!

• Based on what you now know about the marketplace and your job, which of your top ten skills is the most important? Which of your passions can work within your chosen field?

• Do your skills and passions match up with what your chosen target audience is looking for?

Having completed this fifteen-session test, you are to be congratulated. In all truth, you have done more soul-searching and professional analysis than most people have done in the entirety of their lives and careers. And if you are like most of our friends and clients, you feel empowered on a level you've never known before. After all, a clear vision of your skills, talents, and what you can do — not just whom you know or where you went to school — is the real foundation of creating an identify for a career of lifelong success.

With the BAT now behind you, you are in control. You have a clearer, fuller knowledge of your job or business within the context of the marketplace as a whole than you did at the beginning of this chapter. The hard work is done; now comes the fun part. In the next chapter, you reap the fruits of your efforts by sticking your data in the **Skills + Personality/passion + Market needs = Branding Statement** equation and adding it all up for a perfectly brilliant brand!

CHAPTER THREE

The Vision Is Yours

Developing Your Personal Branding Statement (PBS)

Now comes the fun part: All your hard work is about to pay off big. This is where everything comes together in a great way. Everything you learned about yourself (your skills, passions, and personality), all the information you gathered about the marketplace, (including marketplace needs and gaps), and all the work you did on discovering who your target audience is will all be used to create your own PBS. Plus you'll see how people in very different fields and stages of their careers have used the principles in the BAT to brand themselves to move onward and up the career ladder.

However, before we meet these people, we want to talk about one more branding principle to help you develop your PBS. This principle is known as brand positioning. A *product*'s brand position is how people think about a product or service. *Your* brand position will be how people think about you! As we've stated before, if you don't decide how you want your brand to be positioned, others will do it for you: the industry you are in, your boss, your friends, and to a large extent, your enemies. Needless to say, it is better to position yourself rather than have others do it for you — which you obviously understand, or you wouldn't be reading this book.

A good brand position will help guide you in many of your decisions, such as what industry path to follow and what job to take. *The hardest part of deciding your brand position is choosing a single position and pursuing it single-mindedly.* In working with all our clients, this is the most difficult piece of the PBS building process. It seems many of our clients want to be everything to everybody. And it just doesn't work.

For example, a soft drink can't have both the "all-American" position of Coke *and* the "edgy, hip" position of Pepsi. This becomes too confusing for the target audience. Another example of positioning is in the car industry. All cars provide exactly the same benefit: they get the driver and passengers from point A to point B. But you would never know it by the way each car company positions its products: Mercedes is a luxury car, Volvo is a safe car, and Chevrolet is America's car. All have selected a unique, single-minded brand position and have carved out their own lucrative niche. And if you think about it, most successful people have a single-minded brand position, too. That is, most people are famous or well known for one main thing.

So how do you decide which of your many skills and passions you should position your brand around? Simply put, your brand position should be built around whom you're trying to work for—your target audience. As we discussed in Section III of the BAT, your target audience is identified by a combination of demographics, attitude, and behavior. The more you know and understand about your target audience, and what his or her wants and needs are, the better you will be able to position your brand. For you to truly be successful, your skill set needs to match up with what the target audience wants or needs. With this one last piece of advice, it's time to move on to learning more about building your PBS.

THE PBS ORGANIZER

To help in developing a PBS, we use what we call the PBS organizer. This form will help you consolidate all the information gleaned from the fifteen BAT sessions into one concise document, which is, in essence, the recipe for your PBS. Take a minute to read through the organizer. You will be using it at the end of the chapter when you create your own PBS.

Sections of the PBS Organizer	Guide to Completing the Personal Branding Statement Organizer
Field and/or Industry	What is the field or industry in which you have decided to brand yourself?
Target Audience	Whom do you want to reach with your brand message?
Brand Personality	Which of your personality traits and passions you worked with in the BAT will resonate with your target audience?
Brand Insight	What special insight do you have into the target audience's beliefs, habits, or practices?
Brand Position	What is your single most important skill the target audience should know about?
Support	What are the proofs of claims about the brand position that lend credibility to the position?

Do all the sections in the PBS organizer look familiar? They should. They're based on all the work you did during your BAT sessions. If you did your work in chapter two, building your PBS will be that much easier, because you have all the information you need. You just need to decide how it will all work together—how your skills, passions, and personality traits will fit the needs of your target audience.

To help you do your PBS for the first time, we want to share with you a few *Brand Yourself* success stories from all kinds of people in all sorts of career situations from all different fields and show you how they built their PBS. (If you can't wait, you can go directly to page 100 at the end of this chapter and begin working on your own PBS.) The true beauty of applying branding principles is that you can use them no matter what field or industry you elect to pursue, and no matter how long you've been in the workforce — for many years or if you're just starting out. Obviously there will be individual nuances to your branding statement, depending on where you are in your career and the field you select. But the basic principles hold true.

The case histories in this chapter, and throughout the rest of the book, will cover many industries and jobs at every level. By providing a broad spectrum we hope to cover situations to which you may relate. And the PBS that follows each case history in this chapter was crafted according to the following formula: Skills + Personality/Passion + Market Needs = Branding Statement.

Making a Student Statement

Our first example is Joan Morrow, a college student — yes, it's never too early to brand yourself! In fact, the earlier you do brand yourself, the better you will be able to direct your career. When college students brand themselves, they set themselves on a clear career path from the beginning. However, branding yourself when you've been a student is different than if you have been in the workforce. Why? Because students haven't had much in-market experience to use as proof of their skill sets. So they must rely more heavily on two areas: natural skills and academic performance. Or, if they are among the lucky few who know early on the exact field and career they want to pursue, they can begin gaining experience in the field of their choice either as an intern or during summer breaks.

If, however, you're not one of the lucky few, it may take a few tries in landing different jobs and experiencing the "real world" for your true brand to emerge. Don't despair. This is a process, and those who know exactly what they want to do for the rest of their lives before they graduate are the exception, not the rule. However, by doing the work in creating your first PBS, you will have gone a long way in discovering your brand and putting yourself that much farther ahead.

Name: Joan Morrow

Job: Graduate student trying to get into a doctorate program

Career Situation: Joan was a top master's student at a prestigious Eastern university. However, when it came to getting into a Ph.D. program, she wasn't having success. She had been an excellent student with top grades and test scores, but was not accepted at the Ivy League universities. Joan knew she had the qualifications required for acceptance, but still wasn't getting in.

After reviewing Joan's impressive credentials, we concurred that her background was top drawer; in fact, her application essays were among the best we'd seen. The one area where we saw a weakness was this: while Joan's academic qualifications were undeniably strong, there was no focus on her as a researcher, teacher, and—most important of all—published author who would bring credit (and possible grants) to the university where she would receive her doctorate. Joan was focusing on the wrong skills for the target audience she was trying to impress. They wanted to know about her abilities as a researcher and teacher, and she was concentrating on her impressive track record as a student. It sounds simple now, but there was much soul-searching and work done at first—especially on who her target audience was and what they would want from her.

Once Joan had made this discovery, she went back to her top ten skill list and focused on the skill she had listed as her third strongest: demonstrated the makings of a researcher and teacher. She then looked at her proof of claims for this skill:

• published author—published article on organizational behavior and racism's societal impact
• engaging teacher—received highest rating by under-graduate student course taught
• inspiring colleague—students seek her out for comments on papers; served as link between students and senior faculty

Joan was aware of these skills, but felt her academic record was more important, and therefore had highlighted that instead of these equally impressive skills. Once we were comfortable with the new direction Joan was going in, we asked her to first organize everything with the PBS organizer and then to redo her PBS. Her new PBS organizer looked like this:

Sections of the PBS Organizer	Joan Morrow's PBS
Field and/or Industry	Ivy League doctorate program
Target Audience	Admissions boards of all Ivy League schools I am applying to
Brand Personality	Confident, conscientious, and mature
Brand Insight	Admissions boards are very concerned about Ph.D. candidates' abilities to do meaningful, credit-worthy, publishable research and impressive teaching skills

Brand Position	Published academic author, proven teacher, and inspiring colleague
Support	• Published author—published article on organizational behavior and racism's societal impact • Engaging teacher—received highest rating by undergraduate student course taught • Inspiring colleague—students seek her out for comments on papers; served as link between students and senior faculty

Taking all of the information contained in the PBS organizer, Joan was ready to construct her PBS, which takes all the elements in the organizer and consolidates them into a one- or two-sentence statement. Joan's PBS looked like this:

Joan Morrow's PBS

Joan Morrow is a mature, confident doctoral candidate who will bring honor and prestige to any doctorate program with which she will be associated with her already proven skills as a published academic author and engaging teacher.

Based on her new PBS, Joan redid her résumés and sent them out to virtually the same schools that had turned her down for admission the following fall. Based on her previous experience, she was dreading the response; she shouldn't have. Of the seven new and approved applications sent out, five resulted in offers of admission—with fellowships.

Today Joan is putting the finishing touches on her doctoral dissertation at a university with one of the top five programs in her field. Her initial search for a professorship has elicited the interest of several major universities, and she has already gained prominence as a budding star in her academic field.

Making a Corporate Statement

Many people don't quite know how to brand themselves in the corporate world. After all, Fortune 500 companies don't exactly reward mavericks, and with strict policies for dress and other procedures, it may seem difficult to stand out. That said, in some respects it is even more important to brand yourself within a large company since, in most cases, there is more than one person—sometimes thousands of people—doing very nearly the same job. Thus, creating a brand isn't the icing but the cake itself.

Moreover, the good news is that forging your brand statement is, in one sense, actually easier for those of you working for big companies because one of the major components of your PBS—your target audience—has, de facto, already been defined for you. (This can be the firm you work for, your direct boss, or a division head, depending on your circumstances and goals.)

One person who has successfully branded himself in the corporate arena, though he is still waiting for his *Fortune* article, is our longtime friend Doug Gleason.

Name: **Doug Gleason**

Job: **Senior Vice President, Worldwide, MGM Consumer Products**

Career Situation: **Doug has been in business for over seventeen years, moving up the chain of command at such blue-chip companies as Pepsi, Disney, Carnation, and MGM, and readily admits the role branding himself has played in his upwardly mobile movement in the corporate structure.**

"When I started my career at Pepsi, I was, like most newly minted MBAs, an assistant brand manager," Doug explains. "Ironically, though I was a marketing major and even had the word 'brand' in my title, I had never given much thought to branding myself—that is, creating a special slant for myself even in this entry-level role."

But for Doug—and for all smart self-branders—that changed fast. Why? Because as Doug says, "If you don't brand yourself, someone will do it for you—and you may not like the brand that is ultimately assigned to you." Good reason, we think, to intercept others' intentions and forge your own brand, whoever you are and whatever you do!

"I quickly learned that I was competing with some of the smartest people I had ever been around," continues Doug (who himself is no slouch, having earned a Stanford B.A. and an M.B.A. from UCLA). "It became obvious that it wasn't my education or intelligence alone that was going to break me out of the pack, even if they were what got me to Pepsi in the first place. That was certainly the foundation, but I knew that to rise to the top, I needed to distinguish myself in visible, concrete ways."

As Doug completed his first few months at Pepsi, he began to identify a strength in himself he just didn't see in anybody else. Everyone in the marketing department was strong in the left brain/analytical department, but Doug had an additional talent: using his right brain to solve creative issues that shaped the backbone of national marketing campaigns—an especially valuable talent at an image-conscious company like Pepsico. Soon Doug was known as the creative wizard in his group, an attribute that helped form the brand statement he would use in some form or fashion for many more years.

But that was just the beginning. "Another area I found I stood out in was that I had a sense of humor, whereas some of my colleagues took everything dead seriously. I work as hard as anyone, but I could never have made the daily trek from Manhattan to White Plains, New York, if I hadn't thought my job was rewarding and fun. No matter what you do, if you're not enjoying yourself, every day at work can seem like it's a million years long.

"Now I'm not saying I was the class clown or danced on tabletops. But having a sense of humor is instrumental in initiating a sort of camaraderie, and it wasn't long before the people in sales, market research, and product development all wanted to work on my projects because they knew that it wouldn't be just another project to grind out."

By combining a dynamite skill set and acknowledging positive aspects of his personality, Doug was creating a brand—and, in so doing, a fine reputation for himself at Pepsi. Being chosen as one of the first new hires to be promoted was strong proof of that. "Frankly, I don't think I would have been so successful if I hadn't realized my unique skills and tapped into my emerging brand, however 'in progress' it might have been."

And what was his brand? Let's use the PBS organizer to construct it, based on what you've read about Doug so far.

Sections of the PBS Organizer	Doug Gleason's PBS
Field and/or Industry	Marketing for high-profile consumer goods corporations
Target Audience	General manager of a division within a consumer goods corporation
Brand Personality	Committed, gregarious, consensus builder
Brand Insight	Most corporate marketers are analytical, resulting only in solid but uncreative problem solving
Brand Position	Equal part right-brain and left-brain thinker, allowing well-thought-out, creative problem solving

Support	• Excellent analytical skills—created an analytical model to prove display activity is more important than price reduction in moving product
	• Creative problem solver—recommended a completely new way to promote in-store, which resulted in increased sales
	• In all personnel reviews, got an "outstanding" rating for working with people and consensus building
	• Stanford graduate, MBA from UCLA

Taking elements from the PBS organizer, Doug's PBS would be consolidated to:

Doug Gleason's PBS

Doug Gleason is a seasoned marketing executive who can solve any marketing problem using creative and analytical points of view and consensus. A great team builder who is both a right-brain and left-brain thinker, he finds solutions to even the toughest marketing challenges with equal parts commitment and fun.

Not long into his Pepsi tenure, Doug, who wanted to return to the West Coast, nabbed a plum job at Carnation. "My sense of humor and commitment to team building came through in even my earliest interviews," he relates. "When hired, management knew my talents could best be applied, and I could give the most to Carnation, if I were working on what was perceived to be a 'fun' brand. As a result, I always got the most glamorous and festive assignments. The only downside is that they were usually more caloric!" Doug says with a laugh.

Doug's brand has changed very little as he continues to move up in his career. Why? Because it delivers an important benefit his target audience needs.

Making a Health Statement

Branding yourself is equally important for those in the service and health fields. In fact, it may be more important to brand yourself in these fields now than ever before. With ongoing health reform, no one in this industry is immune to losing his or her job. But the stronger your brand position, or the more meaningful your benefit is to your target audience, the less likely you will lose your job. And in the unfortunate event you do lose your job, a strong brand directed at the correct target audience will help you rebound into a new position more quickly.

Another trend is toward hospitals branding themselves to meet the needs of very specific target audiences. These branded hospitals will want to employ those professionals that fit into the hospital's brand.

But even those individuals who have a specialty (which is, in itself, a way to brand yourself) still must compete with other specialists and therefore need to further differentiate themselves. So as we've said before, branding is no longer a luxury; it is a necessity.

Someone in the health field with an eye toward the changes occurring in health care, and with a desire to brand herself and solidify her job security, is Kay Crain.

Name: Kay Crain

Job: Social worker for people with chronic illnesses

Career Situation: Kay has always received marvelous write-ups from her supervisors. But recent state cutbacks in health care–related jobs have made her nervous. Rather than face uncertainty, Kay wanted to ensure that her position is safe by branding herself.

The first thing Kay did was go through all fifteen sessions of the BAT. Due to the uncertainty of her job, Kay focused on the following areas:

1. Surveying her field's history and foreseeable future
2. Considering the competition—its strengths and weaknesses
3. Looking for "gaps" in the market and determining unmet needs

As Kay did her homework about her field of social work for people with chronic illness, she uncovered two valuable pieces of information: 1) despite downsizing, grants were still being awarded for innovative, new programs; and 2) diabetics were often given short shrift, since their condition was not viewed as life-threatening, nor was theirs a trendy disease with a lot of media attention. But there is a large percentage of the population that suffers from the disease.

Kay didn't stop here. She found out that, although limited, there were programs for diabetics, so she didn't think grant money would be forthcoming for another such program. She dug deeper, uncovering more information in the field of diabetes . . . until she discovered a very interesting fact. Although diabetics were afforded some access to a social worker, the needs of their *families* were left unmet. Kay felt that she had uncovered a very real need in which she could become an expert. Kay began to get excited for several reasons: as a compassionate person, she felt she could help a group of people who desperately needed to be heard and understood, and as a professional health worker, she believed she might be able to brand herself, thus securing a space for herself with her employer.

By going through the process outlined in chapter two, Kay now had a basic plan to brand herself: she had identified a "gap" in the marketplace (yes, even humanitarian endeavors like social work have markets), one where she could make excellent use of her skills, interests, and talents. Most important, there was grant money for creating programs that would fill these "gaps." "Why not?" Kay reasoned. "Focusing on diabetes sufferers might lead to an interesting new professional niche."

Kay now set about securing grant money to begin work on a program. She wrote an article about the unmet need she had uncovered and submitted it to a statewide social worker newsletter. She also presented her findings at a widely attended health professional symposium. Now you may be thinking, "Why would Kay do this? Isn't she giving away her brand for other people to copy?" Well, the answer is yes, but by having her name associated with her findings, she's making *herself* the expert, giving her the competitive edge and getting the word out to bring grant funding in.

But Kay didn't stop here: she then sent copies of her speech and a situational brief not only to her boss, but also to the governing board for health services. "I wanted to make sure everyone knew about my findings and that this was my idea," Kay states. In her brief Kay stressed the need for increased funding for social work programs aimed at diabetics and their families. Her argument was so compelling that she was awarded a special grant to test her findings.

Kay's boss was extremely blessed because the grant funds would be funneled into her department, giving the whole department greater exposure and, thanks to Kay, job security.

Kay couldn't help but smile. In a climate where social workers were being downsized and forced to change careers, she had created a new brand—and job longevity—for herself. Here's what Kay's PBS organizer looks like:

Sections of the PBS Organizer	Kay Crain's PBS
Field and/or Industry	Social worker in the health care industry
Target Audience	State board of health sciences
Brand Personality	Compassionate, aggressive, thoughtful
Brand Insight	Services for diabetics are underrepresented in state-sponsored social services and nonexistent for their families
Brand Position	Creator of social work program designed to address the needs of families of diabetics to help them cope with their family member's disease
Support	• Based on industry research, there is an unmet need for families of diabetics to help them cope with their family member's disease • Published author and speaker on how families can cope with a family member's diabetes • Ten years professional experience working with the chronically ill

Kay's PBS, although short, is focused, provides a unique benefit and therefore packs a strong punch:

Kay Crain's PBS

Kay Crain is a compassionate and thoughtful social worker who is an expert in helping families cope with a family member's diabetes.

The end to this story? You've probably already guessed Kay is still employed. That would be reward enough and what Kay had set out to accomplish. But a funny thing happens when you forge a brilliant new brand—people begin to know your name and follow the natural inclination to go after a winner, and more often than not, you end up in a wonderfully welcome new niche. Kay's program has been a success, and she now spends much of her time traveling the state, helping other social service departments set up their own programs.

Making a High-Tech Statement

As little as ten years ago, if you talked to people about the Internet or said our children would be using computers in kindergarten, you would have been laughed at. Today computers are a part of our everyday life, and the Internet is right behind.

In many ways, branding yourself is a bit easier in technology than in other fields. Because this is a relatively new industry, the pool of people with technology industry backgrounds is small. Therefore this industry often must look outside itself and hire people with transferable skills from other fields. Unlike established industries, which require a base knowledge of the industry, technology—as yet—doesn't have this requirement. If you have transferable skills, this can become your brand benefit to a high-tech target audience looking for those skills.

The Internet also provides an excellent way to brand yourself. If you have a "big idea," but little money, the Internet is one place you can make your mark. One person who took her "big idea" to the Internet and branded herself is Jody Seidler.

Name: Jody Seidler

Job: Executive assistant by day, Webmaster by night

Career Situation: Jody has been a secretary at a large corporation for a number of years. Despite her many talents and incredible drive, both the company where she works and her immediate boss will never see her as anything but a secretary. Jody realizes that to move beyond the requisite clerical work, which is the mainstay of her current job, she must look beyond her current employer.

We clearly remember the first time we met Jody, an energetic go-getter. As we explained to her the concept of branding yourself, she stopped us midsentence: "I'm branded, all right. As an executive secretary! And that's the only thing I'll be branded as in this company. And that's why I'm doing what I'm doing," Jody explained. Although we didn't know her exact circumstances, we couldn't disagree with her. Oftentimes, once you brand yourself in one way to a target audience, it is difficult to change your brand to that target audience, because you are providing something they want or need. If you change your brand, you are no longer providing the same benefit.

Many times, to truly change your brand you must also change your target audience. Sometimes this means moving to a different division of your company. Other times it means moving to a completely new industry. Which is exactly what Jody is doing.

Jody's story starts about two years ago. She was going

through an ugly divorce and desperately seeking a support group. "I was a working mom with a four-year-old son. That's all I knew. I now needed to know how to start over," Jody told us. "I also wanted to know how single parents do it all—the homework, the housework—and then go to real work."

Jody's inquisitive nature took her to the Internet. "I searched for a site for single parents and I couldn't find one," Jody remembers. "So I made my own." Powered by the pain, confusion, and anger she felt about her divorce, she became obsessed ("In a good way," Jody is quick to add). She first started with a single home page with simple GIFs, articles and poems written by her, and a listing of legal, therapy, and parenting resources. "I wanted divorced and single parents to know they were not alone, that there was somewhere to turn as they were moving through this painful transition."

With a simple homepage and URL designation (www.makinglemonade.com) Jody went to all the search engines she knew about. She searched for parenting sites, therapy sites, legal sites. She then e-mailed each site and asked them if they would consider linking to her homepage. Although there wasn't a huge response, Jody linked her site with every site that would let her.

"If there had been an e-mailers anonymous, I would have been the poster child, I sent out so many e-mails," Jody enthuses. "But I knew I had to get my site out there. It was part therapy, part mission."

Jody's drive, her "warrior spirit," as she calls it, began to pay off. She responded to everyone who e-mailed her with questions. One day as she was pulling down her e-mail she noticed a very generous offer: a fellow cybercrusader had visited her homepage and wanted to sponsor her site and create—for free!—a real Web site with professional graphics and animation, plus expand her site to include other areas.

"This was a major turning point for me. The dream was becoming real.

"With a great new Web site, I went back to the search engines, located as many sites as possible, and contacted all of them, asking them to link to my site," Jody tells us. "This time the response was amazing." Jody's brand as a "single-parenting authority" was beginning to gel.

Jody continued to respond to all her e-mail, which was growing in volume every day. She now had to update her site weekly, often with her own articles. She became a member of as many Internet and Web site groups as possible. And (funny how this works) she started getting phone calls to be interviewed by newspapers about her site and her views on single parenting.

One day Jody called us very excited. "A Web site—some e-commerce site or something—just contacted me about doing some writing for them," Jody told us. She could clearly sense we didn't share her enthusiasm but couldn't understand why. We asked Jody what her brand was. "To be the single-parent authority on the Web," she immediatcly said. We then asked her how this writing assignment reinforced her brand position. "It really doesn't," Jody stated. "In fact, it distracts from it."

Which was exactly our concern. If Jody had wanted to brand herself as a "Web site writer," the assignment she had been offered would have been great—it would have been another site she could add to her résumé and she could include "experience writing for e-commerce sites" into her skill set. But with the clear, concise brand Jody was beginning to establish, as the single-parent authority on the Web, this assignment did nothing for her.

This is a situation we see often, especially with pcople trying to establish a brand. An opportunity is offered and accepted without thinking about how it takes away or reinforces your brand—which is where our ultimate success will come from. To avoid these types of distractions in the future, we made Jody pull out both her PBS organizer and PBS and told her to keep it handy. Whenever she had a career question, we made her promise to refer to her PBS and ask herself, "Is the career decision I am about to make on strategy with my PBS? That is, does it reinforce my brand?" If it does, great. If not, you probably shouldn't pursue it.

Sections of the PBS Organizer	Jody Seidler's PBS
Field and/or Industry	Internet resource
Target Audience	Single parents and services related to single parenting
Brand Personality	Motivated, driven, with a warrior spirit
Brand Insight	During the painful transition from married to single parent, there is nowhere on the Web to turn to for advice, therapy, or support
Brand Position	The most authoritative, supportive Internet site when it comes to issues of single parenting and making the painful transition from divorce
Support	• Acknowledged expert on single parenting • Obsessive researcher who has contacted and studied almost every available Internet resource concerning legal, therapy, and parenting issues • Experienced the pain and frustration of divorce and single parenting firsthand

Jody's PBS then was consolidated to look like this:

Jody Seidler's PBS

Jody Seidler is the single-parent authority on the Internet. Her real-life experience, motivation, and drive have made her and her Web site, www.makinglemonade.com, the best resource when it comes to group support or legal, therapy, or parenting advice.

Many people have Internet sites. So how do we know Jody has successfully branded herself with her Web site? There are many indications:

- Her Web site gets about 1,500 hits per day.
- She is constantly contacted by both therapists and single parents alike asking for advice or thanking her for the service she is rendering.
- Most recently, a major Web portal contacted her, asking her to build and manage the single-parenting section of their site.

You can visit Jody on her site at www.makinglemonade.com to see how one person branded herself—the high tech way!

Making an Entrepreneurial Statement

Self-employment provides its own set of obstacles and opportunities when it comes to branding. In essence, who you are and what you do blend together. In our experience, passion often plays an equal or more important role as any skill when an entrepreneur builds his or her brand.

The biggest challenge in developing an entrepreneurial brand is appealing to the many constituents that make up your target audience, yet being distinctive enough to stand for something. Those entrepreneurs who find this balance typically find a successful brand for themselves.

Another "must-have" ingredient for the successful entrepreneurial brand is a deep, strong belief in yourself and what you're trying to accomplish. You must be willing to move mountains and never, ever take no for an answer. In fact, this ingredient is so important, we build it into every entrepreneur's PBS we work on.

One entrepreneur who has the right mix of broad appeal and distinct brand style is our friend and client Mindy Rothstein. We wanted to showcase her in this section, because she is the prime example of how a strong entrepreneurial brand can be the difference between success and failure.

Name: Mindy Rothstein

Job: Founder of ROSO, Inc., creator of the Bonding Blanket

Career Situation: Tired of working for someone else, Mindy unleashed her entrepreneurial spirit about two years ago. She created the Bonding Blanket, a patented blanket that allows a mother to "Stay close to your baby, no matter where you are." Great concept—but Mindy's work was just getting started. She needed to get distribution for her blanket and, even though she didn't realize it at the time, brand herself as the CEO of a company that manufactures baby and infant products.

Mindy initially sought Rick out to help her market just her new product. But as she quickly learned, you have to market more than your product; you have to market yourself. "I guess I was a little naive when I started my company," Mindy confides. "I thought I could walk into a buyer's office and walk out with a purchase order. Boy, was I wrong."

Mindy's initial thinking isn't uncommon. After all, most entrepreneurs spend many hours developing their product or service. They are consumed by it. They love it. So when they are ready to go to market, they think everyone else will love their product as much as they do. But it takes more than a great product.

"I did get a warm reception for the blanket from almost every buyer," Mindy tells us. "But I kept thinking, 'If the buyers love my blanket as much as they say they do, then the reason they're not buying must be me.' "

A hard realization, but one that was confirmed by one of the buyers. "I was told that there was a concern that I couldn't deliver the product on time with the huge quantity they needed," Mindy shares. "I realized that until the buyers believed that I could deliver the goods I wouldn't sell so much as one blanket."

Mindy became obsessed with getting her blanket into distribution. She focused on this one missing element in the brand she now started to create for herself. The first thing we did was analyze her market (infant and baby products) and her target audience (infant and baby product buyers). We already knew that these buyers were skeptical of the entrepreneur's ability to successfully meet deadlines. So the first step in branding Mindy would be to eliminate this concern.

To counter concerns of timely delivery in sufficient quantities, we approached well-known local manufacturers with a reputation for on-time performance. Manufacturing expenses would be high, but the benefit of guaranteeing prompt delivery justified the upcharge. Once we secured a contract, Mindy restructured her presentation to the buyers to make this point key.

We also decided it was important to focus on why Mindy had designed her blanket in the first place: she was a working mother, and her anxiety level peaked every morning at 8:00 A.M. as she had to part with her baby and go to work. Who better to create a product like this than someone who had lived through the experience of trying to balance the two worlds of work and motherhood? Most important, based on our research, we knew that most buyers were also mothers and would probably instantly identify with Mindy's plight.

Finally we had to get Mindy used to the idea that she was a CEO. Her demeanor had to convey confidence. Buyers not only had to like her product, but trust that she could deliver. The truth was, Mindy *was* a CEO and had masterfully guided her project thus far. But Mindy didn't feel comfortable in this role, so we had to make her feel at ease with this position. To help, we set up practice buyer meetings, where she would present her blanket and then we would ask the most difficult questions and be reluctant buyers. In time Mindy began to take over the mantle of CEO and became believable, because she now believed in herself.

Mindy's new PBS organizer and PBS follow:

Sections of the PBS Organizer	Mindy Rothstein's PBS
Field and/or Industry	Infant and baby products
Target Audience	Infant and baby product buyers at small to large retailers
Brand Personality	Motherly and caring, but very tenacious
Brand Insight	• Buyers in general are very cautious in what they buy for their stores, but are even more skeptical of first-time entrepreneurs • There is empathy for a working mother • The infant and baby category is ripe for innovation
Brand Position	• Blends a mother's intuition with a CEO's know-how to deliver products mothers and babies love on a timely basis and within budget

Support	• Worked with chemists to create a patented fabric and structured a contract with a well-known local manufacturer to produce product • Created own company to manufacture, market, and distribute product • As a working mother, understands the anxiety associated with leaving a baby to go to work

---

Mindy Rothstein's PBS

Mindy Rothstein is CEO of her own company and creator of the Bonding Blanket. She blends a mother's intuition with a CEO's tenacity to ensure high-quality products mothers and babies will love, and which are manufactured and delivered on time and within budget.

With Mindy's new PBS in place, her buyer presentations could not have gone better. "You know how I thought I would walk into a buyer's office and walk out with a purchase order?" Mindy asks. "That's exactly what happened once I had branded myself! If only I knew way back then what I know now."

Mindy's blanket is in full distribution at a high-end baby specialty store. Now that Mindy has a firm base of distribution, she has moved on to securing additional funds to help grow her business. We think she's grown into her brand of CEO very nicely.

BUILDING YOUR OWN PBS

You've just read about five people who have marvelously branded themselves in all different fields and industries: a graduate student trying to enter a Ph.D. program, a corporate executive moving up the ladder, a health care worker worried about her job, a single parent who is building a career on the Internet, and an inventor who has turned a product into any entrepreneur's dream. But we could have just as well told you about a kindergarten teacher who uses the *Star Wars* movie series to teach his lesson plan, an auto mechanic who calls himself the "car doctor" and makes house calls to "sick" cars in an old ambulance, a corporate executive who continues to soar in the corporate world due to her outstanding reputation for being able to manage up as well as down, or the MTV executive producer who went from cold to hot once he focused on his brand.

The point is simple: you can brand yourself no matter what career path you have selected. So now it's your turn to try. Let's start by remembering our self-branding formula:

Skills + Personality/Passion + Market Needs = Brand Statement.

There is nothing magical in creating your own PBS; it's merely a function of analyzing your skills, committing to your passions, and finding a place in the market that's right for you. So take the time and fill out your PBS organizer:

Sections of the PBS Organizer	Guide to Completing the Personal Branding Statement Organizer Name: _____
Field and/or Industry	*(What is the field or industry in which you have decided to brand yourself?)* _____
Target Audience	*(Who do you want to reach with your brand message, i.e., your boss, head of personnel, a new client?)* ____

Brand Personality	(Which of your personality traits and passions you worked with in the BAT will resonate with your target audience? Pick up to three.) 1. _____ 2. _____ 3. _____
Brand Insight	(What special insight do you have into the target audience's beliefs, habits, or practices? In other words, what need do they have, what gap are they trying to fill?) _____ _____ _____
Brand Position	(What is your single most important skill the target audience should know about? In other words, what is the one skill you have that will best fill the need or gap?) _____ _____ _____
Support	(What are the proofs of claims about the brand position that lend credibility to the position? In other words, provide proof that you indeed have the skill and why it is important in filling the need or gap.) _____ _____ _____ _____ _____ _____

So how did you do? Were you able to fill out each section without any problem? If not, you may want to go back and review any or all of the five examples in the chapter. Or, if you're still having trouble, go back to chapter two and review your personal BAT. All the necessary information to craft a PBS for you is included in the sessions. If you haven't done all the work yet, you may want to go back over those sessions and do them now. It will be worth your time. This is the foundation for the rest of your career. And it really works!

With the PBS organizer filled out, it's now time to write your own PBS. Using the organizer as your guide, you are now going to distill even further the essence of what your brand is. It is important to get this down to one or two sentences so you know exactly what your brand is. So let's take it step by step.

Step one: Start your PBS by writing your name and what you do, or what you want to do. You may want to include some of your personality traits or passions to help in your description. Examples:

Jody Seidler is the single-parent authority on the Internet.

or

Kay Crain is a compassionate and thoughtful social worker.

or

Doug Gleason is a seasoned marketing executive.

or

Joan Morrow is a mature, confident doctoral candidate.

or

Mindy Rothstein is CEO of her own company and creator of the Bonding Blanket.

Now it's your turn:

_____

_____

_____

Step two: Make the statement that provides the evidence that you can accomplish what you have stated in step one. In other words, what is the skill set you have that will allow your target audience to believe you can do what you say you can? This is your brand position. Examples:

For Jody Seidler, the single-parent authority on the Internet: **Her real-life experience, motivation, and drive have made her and her Web site (www.makinglemonade.com) the best resource when it comes to group support, or legal, or therapy, or parenting advice.**

or

For Joan Morrow, the mature, confident doctorate candidate: **A proven track record as a published academic author and engaging teacher.**

or

For Doug Gleason, the seasoned marketing executive: **Can solve any marketing problem using creative and analytical points of view and consensus. A great team builder who is both a right-brain and left-brain thinker, he finds solutions to even the toughest marketing challenges with equal parts commitment and fun.**

or

For Kay Crain, the thoughtful and compassionate social worker: **Is the expert in helping families cope with a family member's diabetes.**

or

For Mindy Rothstein, the CEO of her own company and creator of the Bonding Blanket: **Blends a mother's intuition with a CEO's know-how to deliver products mothers and babies will love on a timely basis within budget.**

Now it's your turn to write down your brand position:

_____

_____

_____

_____

Step three: Now it's time to put it all together. Take what you wrote down in step one and step two, and combine the two into a one- or two-sentence statement. You may want to add a few more "ingredients" from the PBS organizer—such as your target audience—but don't add too much. The whole purpose is to have a very clear, very concise statement that can be supported with elements from the PBS organizer. Before you write your own PBS, let's look one more time at the examples:

> **Joan Morrow** is a mature, confident doctoral candidate who will bring honor and prestige to any doctorate program with which she will be associated with her already proven skills as a published academic author and engaging teacher.
>
> or
>
> **Doug Gleason** is a seasoned marketing executive who can solve any marketing problem using creative and analytical points of view and consensus. A great team builder who is both a right-brain and left-brain thinker, he finds solutions to even the toughest marketing challenges with equal parts commitment and fun.
>
> or
>
> **Kay Crain** is a compassionate and thoughtful social worker who is an expert in helping families cope with a family member's diabetes.
>
> or
>
> **Jody Seidler** is the single-parent authority on the Internet. Her real-life experience, motivation, and drive have made

her Web site, www.makinglemonade.com, the resource when it comes to group support or legal, therapy, or parenting advice.

or

Mindy Rothstein is CEO of her own company and creator of the Bonding Blanket. She blends a mother's intuition with a CEO's tenacity to ensure high-quality products mothers and babies will love, and which are manufactured and delivered on time and within budget.

As you can see, some PBSs are longer than others. Here's the rule of thumb: *a PBS should be no longer than necessary to clearly communicate what your brand is.* With this in mind, try writing your PBS:

_____

_____

_____

_____

_____

If you're having trouble creating your own PBS, chances are you're trying too hard. Go back to steps one and two and review them. Try writing them in different ways until they make sense when you put them together. Don't get frustrated. Take some time off if you need it; then try writing your PBS one more time:

_____

_____

_____

_____

_____

THE POWER OF A PBS

With a crisp, concise PBS you will have clear career direction. You know your strengths. You know who your target audience is. And you know what makes you unique in the marketplace. In other words, you know more than at least 90 percent of your competition. Talk about a competitive edge! And if you're like most people, you soon will begin to feel just how powerful it is to have a PBS. You can use it as a guidepost to make decisions easier. All you have to do is ask yourself, "Is this decision on strategy or off strategy with my PBS?" If the decision is in line with your PBS, it is probably all right to pursue. If the decision doesn't fit into your PBS, it's probably not a good idea to pursue.

Now it's time to learn how to use your PBS to build your career both in the long term and in your everyday life. The next two chapters talk about how you can present yourself to maximize the power of your brand, and how you can get your brand message out to your target audience. You have a brand, and it's time to share it with the world!

CHAPTER FOUR

It's All in the Package

Perfectly Presenting Yourself to the World

We hear it from scores of friends and clients, and we've experienced it in our own careers. "I have a winning PBS, but half the time no one responds to my résumé, or, if I do get my foot in the door, I never get called back. Why don't I get the job?"

People don't get jobs—or, if you're in business for yourself, clients—for a wide range of reasons. Among the most prevalent, however, is that even though your qualifications are well-nigh perfect, your presentation isn't. As superficial as it may sound, how you look, act, and speak is often a deciding factor in whether you will get the job or assignment you seek. If you have your own company, your office, lobby, business card, and even your address is part of the package you present to the world. (Why do you think so many companies scattered all across southern California have a Beverly Hills post office box address?)

In this chapter, we will discuss why packaging your brand—in other words, you—is so important. We will also present case histories of friends, clients, and associates who have packaged their brand with great success.

Yes, judging someone on the way they dress and talk, or the business cards they use may be superficial, but it's the way the world works. The package is what helps sell the product, the employee, the customer. It is an important— nay, integral—part of any brand, and of our personal brand in particular. What's more, we can't begin to broadcast our brand effectively until we know how we're going to package what our brand *is*.

The analogy to the consumer products world has never been more direct than it is here. Like you, packaged-goods companies spend months, often years, researching the market, testing formulations, and conducting consumer focus groups to arrive at the best product possible—just as you have done for your own professional brand. But before spending one cent of what may very well be a multimillion-dollar advertising campaign, before even beginning to contemplate broadcasting this new brand, marketing executives spend month upon month strategizing and testing the product's face to the world: its package.

After all, they may have the greatest new beverage or bathroom cleaner, but no one will be interested unless the package is as compelling as the product itself. Indeed, product managers pick apart every part of a product's label, design, and outer package in much the same way a scientist splits cells in a laboratory. Among the questions he/she asks:

- Is the name right; does it convey the unique benefits of the product?
- Will the logo—its typeface and color scheme—appeal to the key consumer group?
- Does the outer package appropriately frame the product and add to its allure?

Only after these points have been analyzed and tested, and a final package is created, will Procter & Gamble, Colgate-

Palmolive, or any other huge consumer packaged-goods manufacturer even begin to consider implementing programs of advertising, publicity, and sales promotion. So, too, must your package be perfect before you broadcast your brand.

What, then, does your package include? In a sentence, your package comprises all of the visible components of your brand, and how it is presented to your key target groups. Your brand is packaged by your:

1. company's name and logo
2. office and how it is arranged and decorated (even where it's located)
3. business cards and letterhead
4. job title
5. marketing communications
6. personal style, image, and presentation: how you look, act, and speak.

Your present position in the workplace will determine which of these elements you can control: independent workers have the whole ball of wax, while corporate employees have power over some, but not all, of the package elements. For example, you could hardly write a letter to IBM's chairman to ask that the company logo be changed and expect it to have much of an impact. Happily, though, the part of our package that is perhaps the most important—that of our personal style, image, and presentation—is one virtually all of us can manipulate to the betterment of our brand.

Let's look, then, at each component of your brand's package, so that you can learn how to evaluate each element of your own brand to best reflect your PBS.

1. COMPANY'S NAME AND LOGO

What you call your brand has a major impact on how it is perceived. While the choice of a company name is obviously of prime importance to people who work independently—and we'll go there in a minute—it is a less controllable factor for those in corporate life. Though not entirely: you certainly can't choose your company's name (unless you're the founder), but at least you *can* choose your own. Many choose to go from formal to friendly when choosing the names by which they're known. San Francisco psychotherapist and program supervisor Michael J. Ahern has that name on his business card, but his voice mail announces, "Hi. This is Mike Ahern," a greeting he feels puts the caller at ease. "The last thing a psychotherapist wants to do is scare prospective patients off," Mike comments.

So if there's some improvement you feel you can make on your personal name, go right ahead and do it. You can also change how you are perceived through your job title, but we'll cover that specifically later on.

For now, and for those of you who work independently: you need to decide if you want the name of your business or practice to be perceived as authoritative, cute, contemporary, bland, a double entendre, classic, or downright outrageous. Each orientation directly influences how you are perceived by your target audience, and you should give ample consideration to these issues before you select a final name for your company. The tenets of classic brand management dictate that the best-chosen brand name will:

- reflect the nature of the product or service itself
- contain only positive associations
- inspire confidence
- be easy to pronounce and remember

- be distinctive; grab the audience's attention
- have no history of use within the business category that would bestow rights to it on others
- be available for service or trademarking in the appropriate category (the easiest way to find this out is to hire a patent attorney)
- in the best-case scenario, propel the audience to buy

Consider, then, the following business brand names, beginning with the one closest to home.

A Brand Name in the Making: The Write Bank

When David Andrusia, with partner Greg Ptacek, saw the need for a book development company, the two partners subjected their new business idea to the Brand Assessment Test to assess its relevance in the market—that is, whether they had created a viable, attractive, and useful brand. After realizing that they had, they were faced with what is often the hardest (yet also the most fun!) task: what to name the new brand.

Most important is that the name clearly indicate the precise function of the brand. In this case, the brand name needed to achieve the following goals:

- explain the company's function
- indicate the presence of a bank, or a host, of writing talent
- appeal to potential customers' sense of whimsy
- tell the customer what sets the company apart from the competition, and why they should do business with us
- be a name that signals our experience and expertise in the least glamorous (or most difficult) subset of our field. (Note: if it's totally impossible to incorporate this specialty into

your brand name, you can emphasize this talent in other parts of your marketing communication to potential customers — or bosses, if you're on staff in the corporate world.)

With these aims in mind, Ptacek brainstormed the name, The Write Bank. A minor stroke of genius, it achieved all of the above objectives, with one important exception: it didn't convey to the uninitiated just what the firm did. To compensate, we added the tag line, "A book development company," so that editors, agents, and writers — our three major target groups — would understand precisely what The Write Bank was about. In so doing, we achieved the goals stated above. We:

- Explained the company's function through the brand's name and tag line
- Indicated that there was a bank of talent, not just two writers on board
- Appealed to our audience's sense of whimsy by creating the fanciful double entendre of "Write Bank." Who among the real or imagined literati hasn't dreamed of living on the Left Bank in Paris — or, better yet, actually done it? Moreover, the word *right* is always a positive, conveying that target consumers will have made the right choice by selecting our firm (even though it's actually located in Los Angeles!).

A Brand Name in the Making: Hothouse Productions

Consider the case of Robin McKay, a much-in-demand producer who chose the name Hothouse Productions for her firm. "I have never been normal," McKay confides. (Her left-of-center — way left! — résumé, which we share in the next chapter, confirms this view.) "When I was a staff on-air producer at ABC, I always got the 'offbeat' programs to work on, and that suited me just fine. Interestingly, my hip, urban sensibility was much more appreciated by theatrical film distributors and the cable networks, so I chose them as my key markets when I went out on my own."

And whence the name "Hothouse?" "I know I'm breaking one of your cardinal rules," McKay says with a laugh, "but I did so on purpose. As a producer, I've done everything from PBS documentaries to mainstream network promotions to vanity shows for bazillionaires—and I want to remain open to any interesting projects that come my way. For this reason, I didn't want to choose a name or add a tag line that limited me to any of the above.

" 'Hothouse' has an intriguing double meaning," McKay continues. "The most obvious one is of a place where things flourish and grow. But the between-the-lines connotation is of a slightly frenetic, fairly crazy location, and I think that describes my business rather well. It also correlates with one of your other commandments: that the name should be striking and grab someone's attention. Most of my competitors have companies called 'Jane Jacobs Productions,' 'On Air, Inc.,' or other such bland concoctions. I wanted mine to say something completely different, and in fact it's an ice-breaker of sorts.

"Finally," McKay says, "I searched for a name that could be the springboard for a truly disruptive visual on my letter-head and business cards. When my graphic designer presented me with a huge blowup of a rose in a muted halftone, I knew I had struck gold. That was six years ago, and I haven't considered changing my identity—I suppose you would call it my brand—even once."

A Brand Name in the Making: Pen Ultimate Productions

Paul Lauro was a typical, struggling freelance writer who was tired of just making ends meet. "I decided at some point that

I had to stop playing the victim and take the bull by the horns—to consider my writing as a bona fide business and treat it as such," Lauro says. "Before then, I didn't even have real stationery, just the kind of crappy-looking letterhead you get at the neighborhood print shop.

"When a friend who's in graphics offered to design letterhead for me in exchange for taking care of his horrible cat for four weeks, I jumped at the chance. To be truthful, though, I didn't learn till later why it was so important to have a company name and image; I just thought it looked cool. Of course, the first thing my friend asked was, 'What are you calling your company?' and I guffawed. 'Company?' I laughed. 'I work out of my tenement on the Lower East Side.' 'And you always will,' Kevin said, 'until you start thinking of yourself as a going business concern.'

"I was stunned by his insight—far too stunned to come up with a name on the spot, even though writing is my stock-in-trade. 'Uh, let me get back to you on that, okay?' I asked.

"What I did was what I do for other people: I just started free-associating names," Lauro continues. "I sometimes referred to myself as a penman—it sounds like some sort of sport manqué—and I like the word, since actual human handwriting seems to be a dying art. I came up with Pen Ultimate because it's a fun play on words, and ultimately— pardon the pun—says I'm the best at what I do. Plus, I think 'Productions' is kind of cutely self-effacing, since everyone knows writers work alone.

"I toyed with the idea of using a subhead like 'Magazines. Newspapers. Fanzines.' on the letterhead because those media were the bulk of what I did. But I decided not to limit myself. Instead, I put my name, and under it, 'Chief Writer,' which I know is somewhat pretentious, though I hope charmingly so; and anyway, it always sparks conversation.

Finally, a plume separates my name from 'Pen Ultimate Productions,' which I think is a nice design touch."

Many entrepreneurs would agree that the hardest part of getting started is choosing a company name, and it's something that more than one great man and woman have lost sleep over. So take some excellent advice from Bernadette Tracy, founder and president of NetSmart, which consults on motivational psychological research and consumer behavior on the Internet: "NetSmart is a play on the old TV show *Get Smart*, yet I fully realize it's not the catchiest or kickiest name in the history of the world. Frankly, I didn't want something trendy or distracting to the business itself. I feel that what's most important is to make the brand name mean something through your marketing and promotional efforts, be they in the form of advertising, publicity, or a brochure." (We'll talk more about the importance of this kind of advertising in the following chapter.)

2. YOUR OFFICE AS A REFLECTION OF YOUR BRAND

Let's be honest: how many times have you talked to a friend about a job interview . . . and before you even began speaking about the job responsibilities, the people there, or anything else, you critiqued the office itself? Comments like "They have the coolest offices!" to "There's a fully equipped gym!" to "It's on the forty-eighth floor of the General Motors Building and you can see the park all the way to Harlem!" are quite often the first words out of our mouths.

The converse is equally true. Practically everyone we know has, at one time or another, come back from an interview groaning in agony: "Avocado carpeting? What *were* they thinking?" or "They must have bought their battleship gray desks used from the U.S. government" are among the critiques we've heard.

You get the point. Just as employers often make a decision about prospective employees in three minutes flat, so, too, do we "interview" an office or work setting as soon as we walk through the door. Indeed, how a work environment looks is as important as how *you* look is to a prospective client or boss! So doesn't it follow that, to the degree that you can control it, your own work space should be as enticing as possible?

Naturally, your office or work setting should reflect not only your personal taste, but your brand statement as well. Let's say you're a facialist, and you've finally saved enough money to open your place. Terrific! But how, exactly, will your salon look? It could be:

- high-tech (for a sort of Swiss clinic look)
- downtown funky (to lure the model set)
- warm and comfortable (to attract mainstream women who don't want anything too clinical or fancy).

You get the picture. Your office should, of course, be neat and uncluttered, and it should also indicate who you are and what you do.

A Sense of Space: KB Network News

Recently we attended a meeting at the office of KB Network News, one of New York's most respected young publicity firms. (Also, one with a genius brand name: KB comes from the name of the owner, Karine Bakhoum, and Network News makes it sound like a company with something newsy and hot to say—not merely another in-your-face publicity firm.)

First, their location: in the Flatiron Building, that groovily triangular edifice that's one of the most distinctive in the world. Not only is the building unique, but it's smack in the middle of the superhappening Flatiron District, home to photogs, models, hot hair salons, and some of the coolest restaurants in town. (Most publicity firms are on the upscale but unexciting Upper East Side.)

Now, to KB's office itself. We'll go out on a limb and say it is nothing less than one of the most memorable office spaces we've ever seen. The small entryway entices the visitor with a splash of color and framed story placements the agency has amassed in the local and national press. There are no individual offices; indeed, the entire staff sits in one small but meticulously decorated room, with walls kissed by fashion colors and bedecked with still more framed press clips. The message received is clear: this is a progressive, forward-thinking publicity firm that's been remarkably successful with clients in the restaurant business and other fields. Within minutes, we were wishing we could hire KB Network News to publicize our projects, including this book! Our immediate associations were: hip, successful, innovative—winners all around. Shouldn't your office say the same?

A Sense of Space: Sarah Simpson

When David Andrusia first met Sarah Simpson, he was fascinated first by the placidity of her office. In fact, there were just a few neatly arranged papers and a couple of cosmetic shade sheets on her desk. This was especially surprising given her company's reputation as a "sweat shop" demanding extraordinary hours and the surrender of most of one's life. "It's not so bad," he thought. "My current desk is piled sky-high with charts, documents, and ads. I shouldn't have any qualms about working here."

How deceptive was Simpson's office—and how shrewdly she managed her space! By rights, the desk of a director of marketing should have been a war zone. "Sarah," he asked, "you've managed the marketing of a $120 million business with hundreds of SKUs and dozens of new products in the works at any given time—and obviously, you've done so with aplomb. How in the world do you keep your desk and credenza so neat?"

Sarah laughed heartily and said, "You're far from the first person who's asked me that. But you know I was trained as a scientist, and in experiments you must keep each test separate from all others. I have as much, if not more, going on than anyone else here. But since I can only work on one thing at a time, I have no need to clutter my desk to impart a false sense of business. Besides, no one has ever accused anyone here of not having enough to do!"

She continued, "My goal has always been to show everyone—my superiors and reports alike—that I have everything under complete control. Nearly everyone else in this company is flying around like a chicken with its head cut off, while I'd rather give the impression of being calm, cool, and collected."

And that, dear readers, she certainly was. More important, Sarah Simpson taught us an important lesson: unless we're senior executives, it's not in our power to redecorate our offices à la KB Network News, but we can certainly demonstrate mastery of our position by maintaining a neat, orderly, and presentable office space. Nobody was ever impressed by a slob, and only insecure employees believe bedlam shows how important they are to an organization; smart bosses never do.

A Sense of Space: Dr. Randal Digby Haworth

You may well have seen Dr. Randal Haworth on *Entertainment Tonight* or other national television programs. He is a celebrated plastic surgeon who invented the Haworth Lip Technique, boasts a clientele of celebrities and socialites from around the world, and was recently named one of the best eight in his field by *Los Angeles* magazine.

Dr. Haworth's office (which includes full operating facilities) is a perfect reflection of his brand. "It is important for a plastic surgeon to show prospective patients the aesthetic side of his personality without going too far over the edge," he notes. "I am, after all, a board-certified surgeon, and would thus not want to be perceived as a 'fringe personality.'"

This doctor's office strikes an excellent balance: the reception area is warm and welcoming, while the inner offices maintain the requisite clinical feel. Of special note is the fact that Dr. Haworth's own paintings are exhibited through the office and examination rooms. "Part of my brand," Dr. Haworth explains, "is that I am not only a highly trained plastic surgeon, but a man with a highly developed aesthetic sense. In fact," he continues, "I will be exhibiting my work at Bergamot Station (one of Los Angeles's most respected art venues) later this year. This tells patients not only that I have a strong sense of aesthetics and composition, but that I am a well-rounded individual, with interests that extend far beyond the realm of my medical practice."

3. BUSINESS CARDS AND LETTERHEAD

When clients or associates look at your business card, they are not only seeing what you do, but who you are. Your taste, style, and where you stand on the conformity/individuality scale all immediately announce themselves the moment you hand out a card.

First, the bad news: if you're on the staff of a company or any other kind or organization, you have next to no input about your business card, except whether there's a middle initial in your name. If you are stuck with an ugly card or one printed on cheap stock, take heart: many of America's most prestigious companies have ugly business cards. (Think of the old adage about the rich and powerful not having to impress anyone else.)

On the other hand, if you are in business for yourself, you can design whatever kind of business card you desire, and the look of the card directly reflects your brand. Things to consider include:

- *Logo.* Are you—and your business—solid and conservative, or cutting edge? The typeface and logo (if you use one) should reflect this image. If you are an attorney or medical doctor, you may wish a standard, Brooks Brothers–style card. Andrea Candee, a master herbalist, has an elegant, minimalist card that commands respect—as it should, since she is a book author and nationally known authority who has done pioneering work in the herbal field.

- *Size.* Stick to standard-size business cards. Odd or oversize shapes don't fit into anyone's Rolodex or card holder. Period.

- *Stock weight.* Always use a good, strong stock. We realize that this is rather more expensive than the cheap stocks readily available today, but no matter what your business or field, "cheap" and "flimsy" are never good brand attributes.

- *Visual appeal.* Striking business cards capture the fancy of the audience. Every time someone takes ours and says, "Wow—neat card!" we beam—and so do they.

• *Credibility.* Professional business cards and letterhead say, "This is a serious, going concern and the people involved mean business." The mere fact that you have professionally designed stationery and cards means you're a "player" of note. When the authors were marketing chiefs at motion picture studios, we were constantly amazed by the number of consultants and small companies that tried to solicit large contracts with homemade business cards and nary a brochure in sight. Maybe graduates of RISD, Parsons, and other top design schools can work wonders at home on a Mac, but you probably can't—and it can negatively impact your potential for future business contracts when you have cards or letterhead that look like they were crafted by an amateur.

But don't become needlessly distracted when it comes to their design; *the best business cards are those whose design mirrors the raison d'être and/or activities of your consultancy, business, or large firm.* It's truly the thought process that counts, not how much you spend on fancy stock or graphics. We've seen four-color jobs produced by the costliest design firms in town that looked great but, unfortunately, had nothing to do with the business itself. Cards and letterhead aren't museum pieces; their one and only purpose is to communicate your marketing message—and your brand—to the audience at hand.

A good example of a bad business card was one we found momentarily charming, but annoying in the long run. It came from a freelance writer who called his company "Shipshape Inc." and who proffered an expensively produced four-color card in the shape of an anchor. This failed on two counts: first, while "Shipshape" is a fabulous name for a boat-cleaning service, it has nothing to do with promotional writing, which was his field; and, even more egregiously, the anchor, while festive, wouldn't stay put in any known Rolodex or business card holder for more than a minute.

In sum, always make sure your card and letterhead fulfill this litmus test: Does the design and style of the card reflect the nature of my business? An avant-garde look is fine for a fashion designer or record producer, but it would be inappropriate for a lawyer with a blue-chip firm. Always ask yourself if the first, quick impression of the card—its gestalt, if you will—correctly broadcasts your brand. Since this judgment is, obviously, a highly subjective one, we strongly suggest polling sketch designs or mechanicals among trusted colleagues and friends before picking the final one to go to press.

Here are examples of cards we love, and cards that we don't.

The Business Card Review

The Clever Card: The Clever Carriage Company

The best business cards don't just say what a company is, where it is, and what it does; in addition they do something altogether more marketing savvy: they pique the imagination. This is certainly true of one of our all-time favorites, the card from the Clever Carriage Company.

First, the look: turn-of-the-century rough brown card stock that perfectly reflects the mood of the carriage that serves as the company's logo. Then there's the slogan: "For people without wheels." Normally we caution against ambiguity, but here it's done deliberately; one wants to ring Kim up immediately to find out what this mysterious company is all about. (If one did, one would find out this talented merchandiser has developed an upscale shopping cart for urban dwellers who can't take their oversize purchases home in cars.)

What tickles us most, however, is Kim's self-ascribed title—when you're the head of the company, you can call yourself whatever you want—Head Coachman. The entire effect is tantalizing and full of charm, demonstrating C.C.C.'s wonderful sense of flair and style. And with an upscale market like this, a business card should strive never to accomplish anything less.

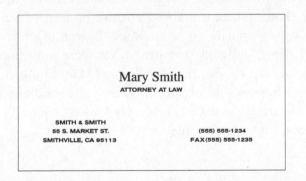

Mary, an attorney, has a clean and simple card printed on a strong, textured ivory stock. Off-white and ivory are always good, elegant choices for people in the professions. There is nothing frivolous about Mary's business card; rather, it brands her as a serious, to-the-point professional.

Printed on transparent plastic stock, this card might be a good choice for someone in a creative profession, but it is highly inappropriate for an attorney. Instead of whispering "Ivy League," it shouts "arriviste." If you were on the lookout for a lawyer, who would you choose, Mary Smith or this lawyer? Besides, the oblong nature of this card means it won't be staying in anyone's Rolodex for long—plus it's a bit too long to fit in most wallets.

A total disaster! What is "Traditional Beauty"? What is a "marketeer"? Why the hundred-dollar bill on the back of the card? (And how tacky is that?) This is, in fact, a promotional items and marketing service, but how would one know that from the laundry list provided at the bottom of the card?

Printed on cheap stock and too large to fit into any Rolodex, this card could hardly be worse.

How do we love this card? Let us count the ways, starting with the company name, Clean Fun. (Don't all companies that use promotional firms want to give their clients just that—fun—and dispense with anything that could possibly be offensive in any way?) Plus, the filmstrip cutout on the top of the card tells the reader instantly that Clean Fun has branded itself for the entertainment industry. However, we admit to being ambivalent about the inclusion of industry association logos, only because they clutter the card and nobody knows what they are; this information would work better on letterhead, but not here. That aside, a totally brilliant business card!

A successful producer, Robin echoes a sentiment we've shared at various places in this book: it's much easier to traffic in ideas that are "out there" when you're an independent consultant or freelancer than while on staff. "I've always been known as a left-of-center creative thinker," Robin says, "a hothouse of ideas, if you will, thus my company's name." We think her business card visually captures the name Hothouse Productions in a striking and memorable way. (Her name and contact information appear on the back of this card.)

The image of a medieval scribe is a charming icon for this advertising "shoppe" and for its copywriter proprietor. Note, however, that Terry lives in Marin County, California, whose denizens are the very sorts who visit Renaissance fairs and take calligraphy lessons. In rough-and-tumble downtown New York or Chicago, this image would be seen as slightly effete, but for upscale, genteel northern California, it works.

4. YOUR JOB TITLE

Sometimes, in the euphoria of a new job or promotion, we're so excited about the new opportunity, higher salary, or bigger office that we forget about one superimportant thing: our job title. "Okay, so I'm still a manager," you say. "At least I got everything else I wanted."

But a title is often more important than you can imagine, for it does much to convey who you are and what you have to offer. There are three main reasons why a job title carries so much weight:

1. *You command respect with the title you have.* This point is obvious: the better the title (VP versus director, director versus manager, manager versus coordinator), the more important you're perceived within and without the company.

2. *To the outside world, a job title serves as an indicator of your experience and résumé.* Those outside your company usually don't have the benefit of dealing with you on a daily basis—so a title helps them understand your daily duties and responsibilities.

3. *Your primary title can be a key component in rebranding yourself.* (We talk more about rebranding in chapter eight.) David serves as a classic example of this home

truth. When he was a director of marketing at a home video company, his boss had recommended his title be changed to executive director, but the president of the company refused, despite having granted David a substantial salary raise. To David, however, the level of his title wasn't as important as what it said about what he *did*. Why? Because he had already set his sights on a higher-level job at a larger company, and knew that advertising and publicity would be part of what an executive director or VP of marketing in his industry needed. For this reason, David went back to his boss and said, "I understand I can't have the executive director title. However, in recognition of my efforts, I would like to have my title changed to director of marketing, advertising, and publicity." David's boss agreed this was a winning solution, and was able to gain approval for this title upgrade from his boss with no problem at all.

It's unfortunate that in large corporations there are all kinds of company policies regarding titular changes, while in small organizations, you often have much more leeway in the title you assume with a new or even your current job. Plus, the rules about job titles do differ slightly for those in business for themselves, and for corporate types, so let's explore each of these issues here.

Small Business Employees/Private Practice

The conventional rule is this: the smaller the company, the bigger the title should be. Thus, if you were a vice president of operations for the Internet division of a huge multinational, but you are now joining a small, upstart new media firm, you'd almost certainly want to be made a senior or executive vice president—and most small employers would have no qualms about gifting you with this title.

On the other hand, we believe that overinflating your title can be slightly ridiculous at best and unbearably pretentious at worst. A twenty-five-year-old with two years of work experience in the publicity field would be an account executive with a top ten public relations firm; with a smallish company, he or she could easily be a senior VP. Nobody's going to be fooled, however, that this person has had a long and majestic career, so what's the point of overblowing the title at this point?

If, however, you are starting your own firm, you have every right to call yourself president, general manager, or whatever other title of importance you like. We find that people are certainly willing to accord respect to those of you who strike out on your own—with all the challenges, responsibilities, and (sometimes) scariness that implies.

Corporate World

It almost goes without saying that those of you who work in the corporate sphere will have far less flexibility in changing your title to reflect your brand. In fact, most large companies have massive rules and regulations on promotions, titles, and other employee matters. The bigger the company, the more intricate the personnel red tape!

What you can do, however, is to *expand* your title to accurately reflect what you do. This is especially important not only with regard to your present work, but to the next job you seek to have down the line.

Like David, Anita Rodriguez is a perfect case in point. Presently she is an ad sales representative for a major Hispanic broadcasting network. But what she really wanted to do is to work in the automotive industry, either in the promotions or marketing area. So she set out a plan to become her company's key contact to the automotive trade as a prelude to changing her title, with an eventual eye on a whole new career.

First she went to her boss with a business expansion plan: "Our shows just don't get the kind of car and truck commercials that the mainstream networks do," Anita explained. "And I think I can change that."

Few bosses would reject out of hand so bold a business plan! "Tell me more," Anita's boss replied. Anita had much to say, and came armed with a plan: "Let me retire all my present accounts and work solely on winning Detroit over to the Hispanic market. Give me six months, and I promise we'll have two of the big three and two foreign advertisers on our side."

That is precisely what Anita did. In fact, after only three months, her boss was so impressed with her progress that Anita had no trouble in changing her title from "Account Manager" to "Account Manager, Automotive Industry."

Now Anita was right on track for her career change. As of this writing, she is sending out her résumé to key players in the car industry, as well as to key promotions firms, and we have absolutely no doubt that she will be employed by one of these companies soon. By expanding her job title within the confines of the corporate world, Anita was able to perfectly position herself not only as an expert in her field now, but in such a way to guide her entire career.

5. MARKETING COMMUNICATIONS

If you are in nearly any kind of business for yourself, you will have occasion to use a brochure, postcard, poster, or direct-mail letter to gain clients. In today's technologically oriented times, a videotape and/or Web site may also be among the tools you use.

The same principles we discussed for business cards (pages 119–122) hold true here as well. So keeping in mind that you want your piece to reflect your brand:

- If your company is high-tech, the look of your materials should be modern and crisp.
- If you run a pet day-care center, they should be warm and fuzzy so that people will trust you to take good care of their animals.
- If you're a hairstylist or own a fashion boutique, your advertising mailers should be uptown chic or downtown trendy, depending on the kind of business you run.
- If you're an accountant, you might have a mezzotone screen of numbers in the background, or a stylized calculator in the design of your marketing piece.
- If you run a catering business, consider doing a photo reprint of some of your most sumptuous spreads.

Whatever your type of business, keep one verb in mind: entice! A mouthwatering dish, fabulous new look, or interesting tag line will be certain to bring customers to you.

Above all, however, you must always remember that the look of your piece, whatever it may be, and the information contained within, *must always reflect your brand*. If it doesn't, your PBS just isn't being put to the best possible use.

We'll talk more about successful marketing communications in the following chapter, which focuses on broadcasting your brand.

6. YOUR PERSONAL PACKAGE

Our research indicates that, at any given time, a good half of the people who should have gotten jobs, assignments, or promotions failed to do so because of the way they look. And we're not talking about extreme cases, that of front men or women whose background and accomplishments may be otherwise impressive but who get plum assignments in a few glamour industries (cosmetics, entertainment, fashion) primarily because of their clothes and looks. We're speaking of the vast majority of corporate and independent workers who were in all other ways supremely qualified for an assignment or job, yet didn't pass Go because the image they projected wasn't dead on.

Now, it's not our intention to rewrite the classic image bible *Color Me Beautiful*, though we're blinded by the brilliance with which its author, Carole Jackson, branded herself to create a multimillion-dollar consulting empire. But we cannot stress enough how important the shiny outer package is to your boss, your boss's boss, or customers you're trying to solicit on your own. Having the wrong personal package can put the death knell on your self-brand, even if all the other components are top-of-the-line.

And while how we look, act, speak, and dress shouldn't serve as our brand in its entirety, they *should* be the finishing touches that seal the deal in delivering our brand to the world.

With this in mind, the following rules apply:

• *Dress for success ... within your brand.* Different industries and companies have different standards of dress. You need to know what the industry or company standard is—it's one important part of knowing everything there is to know about your target audience. For men, it is essential to know not only if suit and tie are de rigueur, but even if colored or striped shirts are acceptable. For women it is just as important to know if a dress will work or if the target audience prefers women in suits. The rule of thumb is, When in doubt, dress conservatively. You can always wear the polka-dot dress or Mickey Mouse tie once you have the job. Match your style to that of the company, whether it's ultraconservative or superchic.

Both authors can recall times when their individuality shot them in the foot:

Rick Haskins went Billy Idol platinum when working as a marketing director at Vidal Sassoon. Even though the company had been purchased by ultraconservative Procter & Gamble, his punked-out hair was considered acceptable because anyone connected with Sassoon was expected to sport an avant-garde look. When Haskins began his search for a position in the movie industry, however, he found brick walls hitting him in the face; it wasn't till a personnel executive said something to him that he realized his hair was holding him back. (Anyone who's ever strolled through Disney's conservative offices knows all too well why this is true.) After dyeing his hair back to its natural brown, Haskins found a marketing position in short order.

David Andrusia faced a similar quandary, though the other way around. Despite the fact that Revlon is, at its core, a fashion- and image-conscious company, the structure and attitude are undeniably corporate. Thus, Andrusia turned up at work in basic Brooks Brothers. After serving his time at Revlon, Andrusia started interviewing with other cosmetics and image-y firms; but, despite ostensibly excellent interviews, no offers were made. Finally, a good friend suggested Andrusia spiff up his image if he wanted to work at Chanel, Lancôme, or The Gap. He did, and snagged a plum position at Swatch Watch USA shortly thereafter.

- **Personal hygiene is a must.** Obviously, a shower the morning of the interview, use of deodorant, clean teeth, and fresh breath are all musts. But you should go beyond the basics. Be you male or female, splurge and get a manicure. Your nails are among the first things people notice. Make sure they are neat and trimmed. If possible, get a haircut a day or two before the interview. Make sure your hair is combed and, if necessary, use hair spray, gel, or some other hair-care product to keep your "do" in place. Men should err on the conservative side of short hair, and women should make sure the hairstyle (both cut and color) is not too outrageous. For women, don't try any new makeup ideas for the interview. Use the makeup you feel most comfortable with and that makes you the most attractive. You need to feel as comfortable as possible.

- **Rest.** We can't emphasize how important it is to look (and feel) well rested. No puffy eyes or black circles allowed. You should get at least eight hours of sleep the night before. And if you normally exercise before work, you should stick to that schedule as well. You need to look and feel every bit the brand that you have created for yourself. Remember: the medium *is* the message. (Recall, if you will, the example of Shandra, the secretary we met in the introduction [page 4], and how she used her personal package to brand herself to wondrous effect.)

But, we can hear you asking, is how one looks so important in *every* field? The answer—how's this for equivocation?—is yes and no. Let's be real: if you work in a grocery store, tromping around the floor in a hypertrendy Jean Paul Gaultier outfit would look ridiculous. That said, there's no reason you shouldn't look as good as you can, regardless of where you work.

Some professions, of course, call for their own special style. Image-conscious companies in New York, Chicago, and San Francisco require both men and women to dress to the nines—though what that means can differ from office to office. If you really don't have a clue what to wear, here's a trick we've both used: simply stand outside the company's building around lunchtime or at 5:00 P.M. and case the outfits as they come parading out the door.

This leads us to a very important point: *always marry your look to the job*. Unless you're applying for a job with a publicity firm representing beauty accounts, a high-fashion company, or a superchic cosmetics company, don't show up wearing Armani or Chanel. The reason, as we're sure you've guessed: it looks like you don't really need the job.

The bottom line is this: in most cases, dress to fit in, whatever that means for that job. Especially for corporate positions, look exactly like your boss, at least in your first time at a new job; later you can push the envelope of your personal style.

If you're a consultant or freelance worker, you have a bit more latitude as to what you wear and how you look. In fact, freelancers in certain fields—graphic design and fashion, for example—are always supposed to look cutting-edge, if not downright avant-garde. On the other hand, if you're a consultant to a stuffy financial concern, you'd do best to mirror the Ivy League look of the key players there. Similarly, if you're a temporary worker in any area of work, it's best to start off conservative and then see how far you can go.

If you own your own business, be it a think tank or a hardware store, you can dress any way you please. But once again, remember that the way you dress *reflects your brand*. A prestigious company that has the big bucks to pay a think tank is going to want its representatives to look comme il faut . . . and wouldn't you rather buy your paint and tools from neat, presentable folks in an organized hardware store than from slobs in a cluttered shop?

Here's the case of a talented writer who combined style *with* substance (always a great formula for success).

The Perfect Package: Karen Tina Harrison

When Karen Tina Harrison left the beauty editorship of a teen magazine to go the freelance journalism and screen-writing route, she saw no immediate reason to brand herself. "Because I enjoyed a certain presence in the field," she relates, "the assignments came quick and fast—almost more than I had time to write. In a sense, there was no need to brand myself, because I had already done so: I was an established and respected writer and editor with ten years' experience in the beauty, fashion, and style areas. My special talent—my brand statement, as you'd call it—is to combine crackerjack writing with a sociological bent, an orientation few others in my field have."

Though savvy and sexy, one thing this talented writer did not have was a memorable trademark—what editors call a "takeaway." "It's no secret that the most successful women in highly visible fields have a beauty quirk or stamp to call their own. Anna's got her sunglasses, Liz Tilberis had her silver bob, and Gwen Stefani has that Bindi dot between her eyes. I wanted a signature, too, though I couldn't think of one shtick that hadn't been tried or one body part others hadn't already pierced.

"Then, at an industry press function," Karen Tina continues, "it struck me that I didn't need an obvious or vulgar trick. I looked around the room and made an astonishing discovery: I was the only woman in a roomful of beauty editors *wearing makeup*! From then on, I decided this would become my signature, and I relish the inherent irony involved. As it turns out, I'm always the most striking woman in the room."

MAKING SURE YOUR PACKAGE IS WORKING

Really, how do you know what others think of the packaging of your brand? While you can consider each applicable element, one by one, as honestly as possible by yourself, being truly subjective about components of one's professional life is difficult enough! Analyzing our personal characteristics is harder still—and sometimes, yes, painful.

An outside opinion always helps. Gather all your marketing materials and take a friend or colleague out to coffee. If you're a freelancer or consultant, you might well want to ask a client you especially trust. In all likelihood you will get very honest opinions from all involved.

Sometimes, of course, you will get unsolicited comments, and unless these are totally mean-spirited, you should take these to heart. At one time a graphic designer David worked with blurted out, "Darlin', are you still using those tacky old business cards? They're so ugly I'll design you new ones for free!" While David was momentarily offended, he did hear what she had to say and accepted her offer. You, too, should seek the advice of trusted allies on your personal package; they are not apt to steer you wrong.

In closing, always take the time to make sure that your personal package—from your business cards to the way you dress—accurately reflects your brand. A few dollars spent on updated marketing materials or an updated wardrobe puts the final touch on your brand package—and in terms of increased business or the way you're perceived by a new or prospective employer, it's an investment we heartily advise.

CHAPTER FIVE

Making Yourself Known
Broadcasting Your Brand

Developing and packaging your own unique brand is a major coup; you're well on your way now to becoming a star in whatever endeavor you choose. But just like a great movie that can't find distribution or a Rembrandt hidden in some dowager's attic, all your work will have been for naught if you don't get your marvelous message out there. In other words, you need to *broadcast your brand*.

So let's cut to the chase and share the methods with which you can achieve great things by communicating your unique appeal—again, by broadcasting your brand.

1. ON YOUR RÉSUMÉ AND IN YOUR COVER LETTER

Of all the avenues for broadcasting your brand, we think none is as important as your résumé and the cover letter you send to prospective employers. The reason is self-evident: if you don't present a winning wrap-up of your PBS at this juncture, you won't even be called in for the interview you seek.

First, your résumé, because that's the easy part. Lord

knows, there are enough résumé-writing books out there, and if you feel unsure about the strength of your résumé, you should certainly consult one of these. We will, however, say this: since your PBS is based above all else on your skills and education, it is imperative that these be listed clearly and concisely on your résumé. But that's not all. Your résumé should also list achievements, and the lack of this vital component is the number one problem of most résumés we see.

Shockingly, even well-educated, highly successful folk often don't seem to get this. Case in point: a friend of ours, a senior sales executive who was just downsized from his electrical parts company's sales force. To be sure, his résumé gave an accurate report of what he did—his skills. It was full of terse, matter-of-fact phrases like:

- Sold electrical parts to major manufacturers nationwide
- Supervised national sales force of fifty managers and sales representatives
- Identified new client prospects

Well, like, duh. Nearly anyone who's worked for any company anywhere knows what a sales director does—and the person to whom our friend sent his résumé certainly did. What the résumé was sorely lacking was a list of achievements, such as:

- Increased annual sales by 30 percent in three-year period
- Streamlined sales force and reduced travel expenses by 23 percent
- Secured contracts from General Motors, Boeing, and Conair
- Opened international markets, winning contracts from Saab (Sweden) and Peugeot (France)

The first set of points merely states the obvious; the second *sells* your qualities to a prospective boss. By the same token, if you are a consultant or freelancer, you should not be timid about blowing your own horn. Are you a copywriter whose ad helped sell ten million bars of soap? A chef who won accolades from your local newspaper or a national magazine? Super—tell the world about it, and your résumé is the place to do it.

So is your cover letter. When we were business executives who constantly needed to add new staff to our teams, we were constantly amazed by the lackluster quality of most cover letters received. While bragging is never appreciated, cover letters represent the perfect opportunity to state your achievements in a compelling way.

Let's look at the wrong way first. Most cover letters are as bland as bread, as in:

Dear Mr. Haskins:

I am writing in regard to the position of administrative assistant advertised in the Los Angeles Times.

I have had three years' experience as a secretary to the general manager of my division. In addition to typing 70 WPM, I can take shorthand and have bookkeeping experience.

I am especially interested in working for Disney because I am a real movie buff. Thank you.

Sincerely,
Carla Clueless

Ho-hum. But how's this for a positive take on the same subject?

Dear Mr. Haskins:

Like every administrative assistant, I'm a fabulous typist and super steno taker. But I can also reorganize departmental files in two weeks' time, help streamline administrative procedures, and serve as a crackerjack personal assistant to my boss.

I am also only two semesters short of an accounting degree at Santa Loma College. Wouldn't my number-crunching skills be another asset in the administrative assistant's role?

I have been an executive secretary at ABC Corp. for the past three years. But I've always believed working in an industry you love is important, and I've been a movie buff (and amateur film critic) all my life.

My superior skills and can-do attitude would allow me to make strong contributions to the smooth sailing of your department. Can we meet at your convenience so that I can tell you more?

Sincerely,
Stacy Sure

See how much difference an inventively written cover letter can make, and how well it can represent Stacy's brand? Her skills, passion, and education are all included here.

If you could use some more help with letter writing, you may want to read David Andrusia's *The Perfect Pitch: How to Sell Yourself for Today's Job Market*. It's full of pitching techniques and cover letters that have helped people win assignments and jobs in a wide range of fields.

2. IN INTERVIEW SITUATIONS

Most folks go to interviews for a job or assignment as if they're expecting to be entertained. They answer questions obligingly, but never really take control of the situation. When you've got a brand, you're not a mere sounding board; instead, you can dazzle your target because *you've got something to say*. How do you use the interview situation to broadcast your brand? The following case histories make this technique crystal clear.

The Job Was His for the Taking:
Benjamin J

His official title is "Activity and Social Function Coordinator," although, as Ben confides, "I'm nothing more than a glorified party planner!" Ben's easygoing demeanor and total honesty are what have made him one of the most successful event planners in Hollywood today.

Ben has worked hard on establishing his business, and he can now bid for events with the biggest names in his field. But like all good branders, rather than compete with the same services and products as everyone else, Ben assessed the marketplace and developed a unique niche for his services and his firm. "There wasn't anyone doing high-end parties exclusively," Ben notes. "Other companies seemed to be all over the board: one day a company picnic for fifty and the next a theatrical premiere for three hundred. Customers couldn't tell exactly what these planners were good at, what their specialty was."

Having gone through our fifteen-day BAT, Ben gained a thorough understanding of himself, his skills, his passion, and his personality. Chief among these:

- His top skill was an ability to take the germ of an idea, however nebulous or crazy, and translate it into something that could actually be executed with élan.
- He was gregarious, genuinely concerned about people, and people liked him back. Ben said, "I was born with the gift of gab, and like Will Rogers, I've never met anyone I didn't like!"
- He loved the finer things in life. He could pick out Waterford from Lalique a mile away!

Based on his personality and skills, we helped Ben craft the following brand statement:

> An out-of-the-box creative thinker who can turn anyone's party ideas into reality and make half-baked ideas spectacular extravaganzas . . . one whose creative concepts and eye, coupled with devotion to detail, have customers coming back for more.

His proof of claims:

- fifteen years' experience with the top caterers and party planners in Los Angeles
- letters of recommendation from caterers, florists, and other vendors
- letters of recommendation from a virtual Who's Who of society and the entertainment world
- impressive portfolio of past events

Target audience: Clients who want to put on high-end social events where money is no object.

Ben had created a niche for himself. He decided to go with a high-end brand strategy, which meant he was targeting a limited but lucrative audience. He had painted a small bull's-eye for himself, but one that, if hit, would reward him richly. Because the total universe of potential clients was small, Ben knew that he couldn't miss a trick; every presentation had to be perfect. "I knew I had but one chance to dazzle," he admits. "I had to make sure I went in with a headful of great ideas and won my targets over. I also knew that, like the parties I planned, the most important thing of all was to make a great first impression."

Before we tell you how Ben handled these interview situations, think how you would handle them yourself if you were in his place. Keep in mind he has a brand promise of delivering fabulous ideas when money is no object, and he is approaching a high-end target. What would you wear to the interview? What accoutrements would you bring? What would you talk about? Ben knew exactly what to do. "I look good in Armani, so that's what I wear. My clients can tell an expensive suit almost before I walk in the door, so I have to deliver. I also get my hair cut a few days before an important meeting—and, because I tend to bite my nails, I get a manicure at the same time. I also go to bed early the night before and abstain from alcohol. This may sound silly," he says, "but it works for me."

We don't think it's silly at all. This is a man who knows his brand and target audience, and understands the importance of first impressions. Before Ben even opens his mouth, he is selling his brand. "I never initiate shaking hands," he continues. "I wait for the client and follow his lead. As introductions are made, I look around the room to find something of interest to comment on, either a painting, a piece of furniture, or anything else that makes sense." Good going, Ben! Before beginning his sales pitch, he is selling his brand by showing the client he knows something about fine paintings or furniture, thus helping to establish his brand from moment one.

"I always carry with me a portfolio of work I have done. It cost an arm and a leg, but it spells success." Another smart move on Ben's part: even his portfolio cover conveys his utterly upscale brand.

"Once I begin to present, I try to listen and understand the type of function the prospective customer wants. And although my heart may be pounding and my head racing, the client never sees me sweat. Instead, I take this energy and turn it into what I do best—coming up with new ideas. I'm pretty good on my feet and can usually come up with a few ideas to get the ball rolling, which establishes me as a creative thinker in the client's eyes." In so doing, Ben delivers on his brand promise of being able to think out of the box and present highly original and executable ideas. It's evident that Ben truly understands how to use his brand statement to his advantage every step of the way.

"Well, fine," we hear you say, "that's an easy example, but what about me? I'm a corporate type and can't brand myself nearly as well because of the confines and structure of the company in which I work." To which we say: Yes, you can! If you've done your homework, you already have a distinguished brand and can make it known even in the corporate world.

The Job Was Hers for the Taking: Dianne DeRenzis

We ran into Dianne, a brand manager herself, at a social function and told her about this book and its contents. She was especially interested in the Brand Assessment Test, as she thought it might give her a leg up on the competition in her corporate world, and asked if she could undergo the program. We were delighted at her interest and agreed at once.

About a month later we heard from an excited Dianne,

who said: "I did the whole BAT as prescribed, and, as I went through the exercises, I began to see how this could really work for me or anybody else. It makes you look at aspects of your personality and career skills you haven't really considered for years," she continued. "I even got a little angry with myself because, as a brand manager, I spend so much time doing this kind of analysis for my products—and have never done this for myself! This was a really good, thought-provoking personal inventory, and I think I've come up with my own dynamite brand."

We think so, too; what she faxed to us was this powerful PBS:

> The brand manager who is expert in turning sick brands into healthy ones, Dianne DeRenzis has over twelve years' experience focusing on brands in trouble. Hard charging and more tenacious than a dog with a bone, Dianne has never been faced with a problem she couldn't solve.

Her proof of claims: Five case histories of brands in trouble that Dianne was able to turn around after coming on board as brand manager.

Target audience: Marketing division heads of major consumer packaged-goods firms.

Dianne's brand statement was clear and concise, with a definite point of difference, clear benefits, substantial proof, and a well-defined target audience that would love the benefits Dianne could provide. We e-mailed her our hearty congratulations, and asked if she had thought how she could use her brand statement in the interviews we were sure she could get.

"I used the BAT for all aspects of the interview," she

related. "I treated myself like a brand and decided the first step was to get to know my target audience. So every company I got an interview with, I called their consumer service line and ordered the annual report. I learned a lot about the type of company I would be interviewing with by the way each report was written, and what was especially highlighted in the body of the text.

"I took this information into account as I prepared for each interview. The more conservative the corporation, the more conservative my dress became. On the other hand, if a company looked to be progressive, my dress style got a little more hip. However, my hair and makeup always stayed the same from interview to interview because I have a hairstyle and makeup that makes me look best.

"When I learned whom I would be interviewing with, I went to a library and ran a NEXIS search to see if there was anything written about that person. The more I knew about my target audience, the more I could target my interview," Dianne said. "On the day of the interview I always arrived ten minutes early. Once the interview began, it was strictly business. I wanted my tenacity and aggressiveness to take center stage. If they liked it, great. If they didn't, it wouldn't be a good fit anyway. And I always made my main brand attribute, that of being able to 'cure' sick brands, the most important topic of all.

"After the interview, the same day if possible, I followed up with a note to everyone I met that day. This usually included the human resources contact, the secretary of the person who interviewed me, as well, of course, as the hiring authority him- or herself. If I didn't hear from the company within a week, I would follow up with a phone call, both because I was interested in getting an update and to reinforce my tenacity," Dianne concluded.

From our perspective, Dianne's use of her brand in an

interview situation wins a perfect 10. She did everything possible to convey her brand statement—even in the kind of stolid corporate setting in which common wisdom says you can't stand out. But that Dianne definitely did. She was a tenacious, problem-solving individual, one whom no company would dare be without.

3. IN YOUR PERSONAL BIOGRAPHY

Once you hit the upper stratum of corporate work, you will definitely need a personal biography. This is used for dissemination to the press, in company profiles, and when you speak on a panel. Similarly, many freelancers and consultants will need to craft a personal biography to let prospective clients know just who they are.

In either case, a personal bio is a great place to use your PBS. This allows you not only to provide the factual part of your brand statement (skills and education), but also the emotional slant (personality and passion).

Naturally, the tone of your biography should reflect the kind of company you work for—or, if you're on your own, the kind of work you seek to do. If, for instance, you are a vice president of operations for a bank, your bio would read something like this:

> Jeanne Montgomery is vice president of operations for Wells Fargo Bank, headquartered in San Francisco. In this role, she is responsible for the management of all technological operations of the bank's branches, as well as employee guidelines, and she oversees adherence to federal regulations in both areas.
>
> Prior to this position, Ms. Montgomery was assistant vice president of operations for Chase Manhattan in New York City. She has held successively responsible posts in the banking industry for twenty years.

A graduate of Wellesley College, where she was elected to Phi Beta Kappa, Ms. Montgomery earned her M.B.A. from the University of Pennsylvania's Wharton School. She is a regional president of Women in Banking and the American Association of Bankers, and lives in Hillsborough, CA, with her husband and two children.

To the point? Certainly. Dry? Yes. But Jeanne Montgomery is a banking executive, not an artist, and this sort of personal bio is de rigueur in her field. "It's lacking in the passion segment," you may argue. Not so: Jeanne's membership in associations in her field is proof positive of her passion for her industry. And while she may well also be into pottery and saving the whales, a corporate-minded bio is not the place to mention these personal passions.

Now, if you're a freelancer, especially one in a creative or technologically oriented profession, you can have much more fun than that. Such as:

Craig Carter redesigned the entire telephone system for Microsoft Corporation—and lived to tell the tale. A telecommunications engineer with a B.S. from Western Washington University, he is also a trained electrician, thus providing a hands-on orientation to complement his academic training. A ski enthusiast and volunteer for the Special Olympics, Craig lives in Seattle with his daughter, Claire.

Get the picture? Craig's bio opens with a winning hook, though it is certainly not flip. He, too, uses all the elements of his PBS, and is able to speak of his passions a bit more directly than is the banking executive, above. (He can talk about skiing; she can't.) Craig's personality comes through clearly with the phrase "and lived to tell the tale," as well as from his skills: an electrician as well as an engineer, he's not afraid to get his hands dirty, something any potential employer would applaud.

4. WHEN ATTENDING CONVENTIONS

We have a friend (name withheld) who always wonders why people who are not as smart, pretty, and well educated as she is get the plum jobs instead of her. The reason: it's not always what you know, but who you know—and, more important, who knows *you*—that can make a huge difference in your career.

Conventions can be excellent career catalysts whether you're an entrepreneur or the corporate type. They are, in short, marvelous forums in which to be seen and heard.

Most people avoid sticking out from the crowd; that's the lemming mentality at work. Let's face it; all of us want to be Madonna, and very few can be. But it doesn't take all that much star quality to stand out at a convention—a little *chutzpah* is fine. Nor do you really have to have anything novel and earth-shattering to say (another fear that deters people from participating). Speak on your specialty on a panel; be a keynote speaker; host an event. In all cases, make the subject of your speech first person, and your work experience immediately comes to the fore.

But don't ever speak in the third person: tell your fellow conventioneers what *you* did to improve security, profits, or morale where you work. That's the kind of information people in the audience will want to hear, and the kind of folk prospective employers like to hire.

It almost goes without saying that these measures are even more vital for freelancers and consultants. You don't want to attend a convention and hand out business cards meekly; be a speaker, participant, or exhibitor, and have prospects coming to *you*.

5. WHEN SPEAKING AT A SALES CONFERENCE

One thing holds true for all sales conferences: no matter how fabulous the location, everyone dreads attending these meetings. Sales reps hate them because they often have to deliver bad news; marketing people have to prepare presentations most attendees sleep through; and throughout the entire ordeal, one has to maintain good cheer.

Here's our advice: buck the prevailing wisdom, and use sales conferences to become a star. Rather than dread them, make your fifteen minutes in the spotlight time in which you become a celebrity.

This can be the case whether you're in sales, finance, administration, marketing, or any other area in your company. Speak with authority, facts, and most of all good cheer. Take every opportunity to allude to people you work with and sales personnel in the field, and extol your efforts as a team. As we stated above, you don't need anything earth-shattering to say. Just speak of your own efforts (always as part of a company-wide team), do it with verve, and people will remember you, if not what you've said.

6. IN YOUR PERSONAL ATTIRE

We've covered this subject at length already as part of your package presentation (see pages 133–137), so rather than our going on ad nauseum, just remember this: *dress for success in your chosen field!*

7. IN WHOM YOU ASSOCIATE WITH

Birds of a feather flock together: this seemingly simplistic adage is the hallmark of the field of social psychology, and makes perfect work sense as well.

Sometimes this can be cruel. Both authors have lost corporate jobs and subsequently been shunned by professional people who we thought were personal friends. It's a common syndrome, in fact. Shortly but sweetly: winners hang around winners, and losers with losers. It's that simple.

Of course, what isn't as simple is what *constitutes* winners and losers—and in the end, it's your life and your point of view that counts. Some prefer to have as friends writers, artists, performers, and other people who create, even if they live in genteel poverty, while others may see money as the end-all and be-all, and don't wish to hang around folk who can't afford to eat at fancy restaurants or dress in designer styles.

The choice is yours, but regardless of the route you choose, the kind of people you hang around can be a direct reflection of your PBS. Case in point:

Helene was an account executive for a brokerage firm. She consistently sold in the top 10 percent of her group and was a member of a local women's broker group. However, she believed her work was her work, and her personal life was her personal life: an aspiring artist, Helene chose as her personal friends downtown types, and not the yuppies at her firm. When she was twice passed over for a sales management post, Helene asked her boss why. "You're a great performer," he admitted, "but you're just not perceived as one of the team." Helen was outraged at first—hadn't her numbers been top-of-the-line?—but then she realized what her boss was saying: she wasn't a broker at heart; she'd rather have spent evenings alone than with her colleagues, who shared none of her interests. The choice was obvious: become a company woman and get the promotion, or follow her dreams. Helene did the latter. She saved six months' salary, quit her job, and pursued her singing full-time.

Who you're seen with is undeniably important if you're in the corporate world. Are you with the fast-trackers, the "in" crowd (yes, companies are very much like junior high school), the hardworking, seen-but-not-heard set; or with the grousers, complainers, and iconoclasts?

As we've said repeatedly, the self-knowledge you gain through awareness of your PBS is sometimes striking, and it certainly is when it comes to those with whom you associate. Many of our clients have had "Eureka!" moments in precisely this regard. If you, like Helene, come to realize that your working life is very much different from who you really are, this may well be a signal that you're in the wrong field. This would be a good time to take stock of the "passions and personality" part of your PBS equation, with an eye toward redirecting your career to a place more compatible with your personal affinities, interests, and style. Why settle for a meal ticket when work can be invigorating and rewarding as well? (You'll find chapter ten, on rebranding yourself, a good place to start.)

8. IN BROCHURES AND OTHER MARKETING COMMUNICATIONS

Brochures, newsletters, ads, press releases, trade publications: all are highly visible reflections of your brand, and they are among the most important tangibles required to successfully broadcast your brand. As such, they should be given thoughtful attention.

Even more than business cards and letterhead, which must convey your brand in one brief visual image, these longer marketing communications can make your Personal Branding Statement crystal clear. They are a wonderful opportunity to tell your audience who you are and what you can do—preferably better than anyone else.

Think about this: how many times have you received a newsletter or brochure and seen nothing but a mass of words densely populating a (sometimes poorly printed) page? We get these all the time—in banks, in the mail, at work, and in leaflets distributed on the street—and usually we toss them away immediately.

Consider, on the other hand, the flip side of the coin: those brochures, mailings, and ads that actually make us smile. Bright graphics, interesting topics, and a distinctive visual style are the elements that make us read and react to the marketing materials we receive many times each day.

Yes, bright and beautiful is wonderful, but it's only half the story. When preparing these documents, among the issues you should be considering are the selfsame ones you used with your own focus groups to develop your brand. The most important ones are:

• Does the marketing material (press release, brochure, bio) make my brand crystal clear?

• Does it emphasize one major point of difference—one unique position—and, where applicable, offer proof of this talent or skill?

• Are secondary/tertiary selling points mentioned in a cogent, easy-to-grasp way?

• Are the five ws of journalism—who, what, when, where, why—stated concisely within the body of the brochure, Web site, or press release?

• Most important, does this material relate the key points

of my Personal Branding Statement in a way that people will see precisely what I offer—and why I'm different from and better than competitors in my field?

With this in mind, let's consider the brand broadcasting techniques—pitch letters and brochures—that can work hardest for you. But before proceeding, we'll address one valid concern many of our clients share: "These methods may work great for people who are self-employed, but how can I use these in my corporate job?"

The answer is elementary, dear Watson. An analogy for each of the following brand broadcasters exists, even if you work in the stodgiest blue-chip firm. For example, if you work for a big company, you're obviously not going to create a brochure; it would be presumptuous, and besides, you don't need to solicit clients per se.

But think for a minute. What, really, is the aim of a brochure? To get new customers, yes, but also to advise the public of what you do. In the corporate case, doesn't it make good sense that you should keep your boss and/or other big-wigs advised of what you do—and why you're better than your colleagues? Of course it does, which is why you should be writing a monthly status report and, if it exists, contributing to your company newsletter without a moment's hesitation. Think higher-ups don't read these newsletters? Think again; they most certainly do, and shouldn't your name—and brand—be on the tip of everyone's tongue?

Now let's cover some of the many possibilities open to you in broadcasting your brand:

a. Pitch Letters

Of all the ways in which you'll broadcast your brand, the most common, and thus, most useful, is the pitch letter.

Whether you're looking for a new position or prospecting for new clients for your business, you can use your Personal Branding Statement almost verbatim in letter form.

More important still is the fact that, when it comes to a pitch letter, you're the master of your fate. We've seen how highly successful self-branders used interview situations to their great benefit, and a little later you'll see how you can use other marketing tools to communicate your brand. But none puts you in the driver's seat as fully as the pitch letter, because it allows you to state your brand in a clear, straight-forward fashion that your target will understand in an instant.

This is true whether you're a corporate employee or are self-employed. Let's revisit our friend Dianne DeRenzis (page 146) to illustrate the former case. As you'll recall, Dianne's specialty is turning around ailing brands. While looking for a new job, she found a near-perfect want ad: a company looking for a senior product manager on a long-standing dog food brand.

Dianne was the last person in the world to just send off her résumé into the great want-ad void. She knew that to get the job she deserved, she needed to establish her brand—and, through the following letter, did so with élan:

Ms. Uma N. Resources
Future Employer
111 Giant Plaza Way
New York, NY 10000

Dear Ms. Resources:
    When a brand is losing market share at a rate of 10 percent, you need more than just another product manager. You need a "brand doctor," and such a one is me.

I know, because fixing ailing brands was my specialty at Fido Foods, where I halted the further demise of a failing brand—and actually posted a 3 percent sales increase in less than three months' time.

How did I do it? Not by any quick fix, but through a strategic repositioning of the brand, one that in this case has resulted in an overall sales increase of 10 percent over the past fiscal year. (This is a statistic I'm especially proud of, since two other product managers had tried unsuccessfully to do the same—thus my "brand doctor" tag!)

Strategic excellence is paramount, to be sure, but so are tenacity and perseverance. All three are qualities I possess in abundance and would allow me to effect the turnaround of your Yummy Treats brand.

My résumé is attached for your review. In addition, I have taken the liberty of asking Janet Dawson, a mutual former colleague, to call you to discuss my background further with you.

I look forward to meeting at your earliest opportunity, and to discussing how to turn Yummy Treats into the winner it deserves to be.

Sincerely,

Dianne DeRenzis

Now, tell the truth. If you were the hiring authority, would you place Dianne's résumé anywhere except at the top of the heap? Of course not! And that should be your goal in using pitch letters to get interviews for a consultancy or full-time job. Just as Dianne did, refer to your brand statement (which should be posted prominently above your computer) before, during, and after any pitch letter you write.

Incidentally, if you feel the proposition you make in your pitch is too weak, this may reflect one or more failings on the part of your brand. If this is the case—that is, if you really can't convey to a prospective employer precisely what sets you apart and why you should be hired—you may want to rethink your brand. Chapter seven is where we show you how to do just that.

Of course, if you're self-employed, you can also use a pitch letter to state your brand loud and clear. Paul Lauro, the freelance writer profiled on pages 113–115, took the Brand Assessment Test and developed a brilliant brand: a music industry writer who is a ten-year veteran of alternative bands. With this position and key music press targets in hand, writing a pitch letter—something he'd previously viewed as a chore—became a breeze. The following pitch got Paul assignments galore:

Ms. Courtney Dove
Editor-in-Chief
HOLE MAGAZINE
San Francisco, CA

Dear Ms. Dove:
Time was, rock magazines were all about music. Today, sadly, they seem to be obsessed with gossip and fashion more than riffs and chords.
But it doesn't have to be that way.
I know what your readers want because I'm one of them. They want stories on their favorite recording artists' music, lyrics, and the creative process . . . and I'm just the man to give it to them.
A ten-year veteran of various and sundry bands (none

---

of which you've ever heard of, alas!), I know what the music in the music industry means. And having contributed to such publications as Melody Maker, Spin, *and* Rolling Stone *(clips enclosed), I can combine journalistic élan with the insider's knowledge only a musician can provide.*

I think your readers would love to know more about the power punk revival movement in Kansas—yes, Kansas!—and HOLE *would be the first magazine to scoop this trend. If this strikes your fancy, please call me at 212/555-5555.*

Best and thanks,

Paul Lauro

b. Brochures

It could be a glossy brochure, if you've got the bucks . . . a two-page foldout for smaller concerns . . . or a Xeroxed flier for fledgling "firms." Whatever the medium, the message should be the same: My business is (apartment cleaning, public advocacy, roofing, computer consulting), and X, Y, and Z reflect my Personal Branding Statement—the supporting skills and proofs that tell consumers why they should call me and nobody else.

In writing and designing brochures, don't get fancy until you've covered the basics. Always make sure your brochure:

• *Establishes the nature of your business.* This sounds quite obvious, but as consumers we've seen many brochures that were totally oblique. People look at direct-mail pieces for mere seconds before tossing them, so you have to make your brand known in a flash. For example, the brochure of Jody, our Internet single-parent authority, had a headline that read: "Tired of Having No One to Talk to? Come Talk to Us!" This immediately told prospective consumers what she could do; it made an interesting proposition on the spot.

• *Tells people specifically what services/products you offer.* After you've made the initial proposition, you must provide the specifics that set your business apart. Here, Jody told exactly what kinds of services she could provide on the spot, what legal, therapy, and other resources she had, and other particulars of how her Web site worked.

• *Offers testimonials/client list.* Absolutely key! Tell who else you've worked for, especially if they're names people know (either nationally, like IBM and Clairol, or within your community, say, Tom's Bakery or Mayor Johnetta Jones). People want a company they can trust, and that others have trusted before them.

• *Provides your background.* What is your training and education; where else have you worked; what experience do you have that makes you an authority in the field? Jody, for instance, wrote that "I know the pain and loneliness of divorce, and vowed no one would have to go through what I did alone—ever again."

With your goal in mind, let's read what Jody wrote to get out the word on her newly popular Web site:

Ms. Dee Jacobs
Lifestyle Editor
City Times
Los Angeles, CA

Dear Ms. Jacobs:
   There is nothing more painful than the lonely feeling a divorce can bring on—and having nowhere to turn and no one to talk to. I know; I lived through it. But just barely. I didn't know where to get information or where to turn for support.
   Which is why I created www.makinglemonade.com, *the best Internet site for single parents looking for support or a resource of everything they need to know pre, during, and post a divorce. My site specializes in divorces where children are involved and the special needs of single parents.*
   With the divorce rate as high as it is, wouldn't your readers be interested in knowing more about this valuable resource? I'd love to talk to you about the many exciting programs we have. Or you can visit the site yourself at www.makinglemonade.com *and leave me an e-mail message.*
                    Best and thanks,

                    Jody Seidler

Now this is a letter guaranteed to get a call—and, ultimately, a feature article. You, too, could easily get the kind of visibility you're seeking if you craft a letter like this.

9. WHEN CONTACTING THE TRADE OR CONSUMER PRESS

Smart professionals in every field know that using the press can help make their names known. Whether you are seeking to be mentioned in a trade publication (like *Woodworking News*) or the consumer media (*Chicago Tribune*, ABC Evening News), your approach should be the same: make sure your press communications establish exactly why you're unique—and deserving of press—by establishing your brand.

The Consumer Media

Don't doubt that some newspaper will print a story on you. That attitude may have been based on the truth in the past—but now *you've branded yourself*. You're no longer just another paralegal or computer consultant or real estate agent. *You have a brand.* Remember Jonelle, the CPA who "put words behind the numbers" ... and Alejandro, who invented "Alerobics"? They weren't just workers in their fields; they became innovators and specialists by dint of their brands. And if breaking away from the herd is your goal, so, too, should you.

Why would a newspaper or TV station possibly be interested in what you do? Because the best branders don't just exist; they create. Benjamin J wasn't just a "glorified party planner"; he developed and marketed his own high-end firm.

All you need to do to get started is to write a clever cover letter to the following folks:

- Features editors at local papers (both major metro dailies and free weeklies)
- Lifestyle or business editors at the same kinds of papers

• Assignment editors at the local TV stations (but don't waste your time with the national evening news programs unless you've got earth-shattering news in your field)

• Producers of radio programs. To know what station is right for your brand, listen to your local stations and get a sense of who does what. (Usually radio stations are best for business, health, and socioeconomic issues.)

Trade Magazines

In our first professional positions, we marveled at the incredibly successful people who graced the pages of our industries' trade magazines. We're talking about the folks thought important enough to be quoted in articles, who were photographed at industry functions, and who were even asked to contribute short pieces to the body of the magazine. It took us several years to figure it out, but we're here to tell you they weren't chosen by God above to shine. No, they were the masters of their own fate. Nobody made them stars except themselves.

And you can do the same. Virtually every trade or profession has one or more trade publications that you should view as your own personal vehicles for broadcasting your brand. How do you do it? Let us count the ways:

1. To garner citations, write to the magazine's editor-in-chief and let him/her know you'd be happy to voice your opinion in future articles on your area of expertise. This is important for on-staffers and absolutely crucial for those who are self-employed since it's nothing less than the best publicity they can get.

2. To assure getting your mug shot in the trades, always stay au courant with the goings-on in your field. Attend par-

ties, conferences, and other functions to make your presence known!

3. To grab great bylines, write to the editors and ask to write a short piece on a subject of interest in your field. Trade editors love receiving submissions from people working in the industry that their magazine covers, to round out the pieces their own reporters write.

MAKING A VISIBLE IMPACT

You see now how many routes you can take to package and broadcast your brand to let the world know just how accomplished you are, and what truly sets you apart from the pack. In the next chapter, we discuss how to use your personal brand to forge new professional paths, whether you are in the corporate world, are in business for yourself, or are just making the move to strike out on your own.

CHAPTER SIX

Branding Yourself to Get That Promotion

Branding yourself helps to ensure career success, and for most people, this translates into three things: 1) job security; 2) fair pay for the job you do; and 3) recognition for a job well done in the form of pay raises and/or promotions. In this chapter we will explore how branding can help you achieve these success factors in the corporate world.

GETTING AHEAD

In most large companies, unless you are the CEO, CFO, or president, there is probably more than one person—sometimes thousands of people—doing very nearly your same job, with very nearly the same, if not *the* same, job title. Thus, creating a brand and setting yourself apart from the crowd isn't the icing but the cake itself within the corporate world.

Luckily, forging your brand statement is, in one sense, actually easier to do if you work in a corporation. Specifically, in a corporation, your target audience—one of the major components of your PBS—has, de facto, already been defined for you. It is usually either the firm you work for, your direct boss, or a division head, depending on your circumstances and goals. And to figure out how to move ahead in your job, you need look no further than your nearest business magazine.

Go to the nearest bookstore that stocks periodicals and pick up a copy of the latest *Fortune* or *Forbes*. When you come to an article about a large company's CEO, head of sales, director of product development or some other department, read the first paragraph. Almost always, the writer will use three to four words or phrases to describe the subject of the article: "hard charging," "cost conscious," "people savvy." These phrases are more than just descriptions; these traits, skills, and/or passions are generally why the subject of the article got to where they are. In other words, this description is their brand!

So how do *you* get from your current middle-of-the-road position to *Fortune* magazine cover story? The way to start is to make sure you have the correct PBS. That is, are your skills and passions meeting the needs of the market and your target audience? (We keep coming back to this, but like a good architect we know masterpiece buildings begin with master blueprints.)

If you feel uncomfortable with any one of your PBS building-block components, you may want to go back to chapter two and review corresponding sections of the BAT. However, if you know and are comfortable with your brand, let's see how to make your brand work for you in the corporate world.

Until now all of our suggestions have all been in the affirmative, telling you what to do. To brand yourself in a corporation, we're going to take a slightly different tack and tell you what three things *not* to do.

THREE THINGS NOT TO DO:

1. Don't wait for the opportunity to demonstrate your brand; *create* the opportunity.

2. Don't be afraid to stand out—whether in how you dress, how you think, or by the risks you take.

3. Don't try to be everything to everybody; instead, focus on a specific need of your boss or target audience and then do everything within your brand to meet that need.

Let's look at each point in detail.

DON'T WAIT FOR THE OPPORTUNITY TO DEMONSTRATE YOUR BRAND; *CREATE* THE OPPORTUNITY

Many people make this mistake, especially those new to the corporate world. They tend to wait to be told what to do, rather than proactively demonstrate their unique skills. "Taking the initiative to make things happen is critical for success, in or out of a corporation," states executive recruiter Heath Smith. "You need to show what you're made of or realize you may be risking your only chance to shine."

We couldn't agree more. You simply can't wait for someone to ask you what you are good at. You have to create your own opportunities. A starting point may be examining what you do every day in your job and then comparing these tasks to your job description. Are there any elements in your job description that aren't getting done? If so, you may want to start incorporating those tasks into your job.

Or is there a special project that you want to do—and you think would highlight your brand position—but isn't within your job description? Take the initiative and do it anyway.

This may mean working after hours or in between assigned projects, but the extra work is well worth the effort if it means the difference between creating a brand for yourself or not. Someone who learned this lesson is Scott James.

Taking Initiative: Scott James

We first met Scott on a Saturday at lunch, his invitation. In his job as a manufacturing traffic coordinator, Scott was responsible for the coordination of what packaging and parts needed to be ordered and manufactured to keep the pipeline full enough for sales orders to be filled on a timely basis. Scott's job was fairly demanding, and required the skill sets of attention to detail and ability to analyze numbers. Obviously we were curious to see why Scott had asked us to lunch.

Like all good manufacturing executives, Scott got right to the point: "I want you to brand me. I feel like I know the company, understand my job, and do it well . . . at least, there haven't been any complaints. But I'm not really sure what I need to do to get promoted. Can you help me?"

Scott's request was typical, especially for someone relatively new to a corporate environment: he was anxious to be promoted quickly but did not quite know the ground rules.

After reviewing the results from Scott's BAT, his résumé, and his job description, we surmised that there was a good fit between Scott's skills and personality and the job he had selected. Further, Scott seemed to have a good relationship with his boss. There didn't appear to be any obstacles Scott would have to overcome prior to a promotion from a branding perspective.

Where things got a bit tricky was with the history of departmental promotions and corporate policies at his company. There was no correlation between time on the job and promotion, which is unusual, especially in a corporation.

The one piece of information that gave us a starting place was this: even though Scott worked at a midsize corporation with over $100 million in sales, only the president of the company could authorize promotions. Unusual, yes. Insurmountable, no.

We asked Scott if he ever came in contact with the president. Scott told us the only time he was in the same room with the president was at the manufacturing update meetings held every week for an hour. With this last piece of data we set our strategy in place:

1. To get promoted, Scott would switch his target audience from his direct boss to the president of the company.

2. Scott had only one hour each week in which he could impress the president with his unique brand.

3. Scott needed to focus on the needs of the president and see if there was anything the president wanted but wasn't getting from anyone else.

4. Rather than wait for an opportunity to perform, he would *create* the opportunity based on what was being discussed in the weekly manufacturing update meetings.

Scott agreed to start paying special attention in his weekly manufacturing update meetings and see if there was a repeated request from the president not being handled. He also agreed to view these meetings from the perspective of his target audience, the president, and ask himself this question: If he were president, what would he want out of these meetings?

For the first few weeks, Scott didn't hear about any opportunities; he became anxious and voiced a concern that an opportunity might never present itself. But we knew differently: in every job in every corporation, there is always more work than gets done. Eventually an important task would present itself.

Then, within a month, for two weeks in a row, the same topic was discussed, but no decisions made. The company offered a special "bonus" pack (a package which contained 50 percent more product for the regular price) that the sales force loved because it was easy to sell. But manufacturing didn't like it because they had to shut down the plant and reconfigure the manufacturing lines to fit the different size of the special package. The president asked if the company was making money on the bonus pack.

Sales said yes, but didn't have specific data to prove their point.

Manufacturing said no, but didn't have specific data to prove their point.

We said "Great," because we had found a need Scott could fill. A game plan was set: Scott would be proactive and do an analysis on the bonus pack and resolving once and for all whether it was profitable for the company. Although Scott hadn't been asked specifically to do an analysis, we felt this was an excellent way to position Scott to the president, his target audience. Further, Scott would be providing an answer the president was looking for and that no one was providing. And, because analysis was in Scott's skill set and part of his PBS, he could keep his PBS, with which he felt very comfortable.

Scott's PBS was this:

Scott James's PBS

Scott's precise—almost maniacal—attention to detail and superior analytical skills allow him to schedule and produce the correct product at the right quantity on a timely and cost-efficient basis.

But prior to Scott's getting started, we suggested one more thing: he needed to cover what he was doing with his direct boss. Scott had to do this for several reasons. First, it was important to get his boss's "buy-in" so there would be no surprises. Second, his boss needed to be assured that Scott would be doing the analysis on his own time and that his regular work wouldn't suffer. And third, it was important that Scott's boss also see his proactive nature.

As traffic coordinator, Scott had access to the sales department's data, including shipments to the accounts and sell-through to the consumer at the accounts. After getting his boss's support, Scott worked on the analysis for three to four hours every night after work and on Saturday. He compiled charts and graphs and looked at the numbers many different ways. He knew how important this was to his career and realized this might be his only chance to impress the president for a long time.

By the next manufacturing update meeting, Scott was ready with his presentation. He had printed enough copies for everyone in attendance and had practiced his verbal presentation in front of the mirror. He also read through his PBS beforehand for confidence and clarity.

Sure enough, the topic of the bonus pack came up. But this time, rather than no one having an answer, Scott took his cue and told the meeting he had done an analysis of the situation, which he would like to discuss now. And with that introduction, he passed out the presentation.

Scott told us later he doesn't really remember everything he said, but he was so well prepared he knew every point he wanted to make. "By the time I finished, everyone was looking at my charts and the president was smiling," Scott gleefully reported. "I had done my best and felt really good about the whole process." Scott had taken control of his career and created an opportunity for himself to shine, rather than waiting for an opportunity. He had made himself known to his target audience and presented his brand in an effective manner. We couldn't ask for more.

Shortly after the meeting, Rick ran into Scott at corporate headquarters. Scott was with someone Rick didn't recognize. As it turns out, Scott could add one more skill to his list: training his replacement! Scott had been promoted. Now he had the president's ear concerning what special packs the company should and shouldn't be manufacturing—and all because of his analysis!

DON'T BE AFRAID TO STAND OUT

Corporate protocol, such as dress codes, set procedures, and other rules and regulations, are how a large corporation maintains a systematized approach to doing business. But compliance to this protocol doesn't mean you can't be an individual. Many of the most successful corporate professionals we know toe the company line, but don't give up their individuality to do it. And the differences you display could end up being your strongest assets.

The three areas where you can stand out most are in the way you dress, the way you think, and the risks you take. The farther you stray from corporate or industry norms, the more vulnerable you become, *but if done with the right PBS for the right target audience, you can expect success*. We're not suggesting you break corporate rules or go beyond set boundaries. For example, if dress codes call for women to wear dresses only, you shouldn't push beyond the limit by wearing pants. Or if you work in a library, we don't suggest you replace the classics with Cliffs Notes. Yes, you would stand out, but you'd probably also be thrown out. We are suggesting that thinking differently, and taking calculated risks, can help you create a niche for yourself—even in corporate America.

The next two people branded themselves within their corporations' set guidelines, but weren't afraid to stand out.

Standing Out from His Peers: Jonathan Weedman

"My job is my passion. I love my work, I love my company," says Jonathan, vice president for the Wells Fargo Foundation, the nonprofit and donation arm of Wells Fargo Bank. Jonathan loves every minute of his dream job: "When you have something you really love, the worst thing that could happen is losing it. To make sure that doesn't happen with my job, I put in a full day's work and then some." What corporation wouldn't want an employee with this much drive and enthusiasm?

Early on, Jonathan was working for Wells Fargo Bank, and his training focused on how to acquire small-business accounts for the bank. He would call on small to midsize businesses in the Los Angeles area, and while he enjoyed his job and liked his company, he felt he had not distinguished himself from his peers, all of whom were calling on essentially the same accounts.

"One day I was looking through the Yellow Pages when I saw an ad for a business that was 'gay owned and operated,'" Jonathan recalls. "I looked at the ad and thought to myself, 'Why shouldn't I call on gay businesses?'" Jonathan, openly gay at work, knew that no one, either from his bank or from the competitive banks, was calling on this particular group. And although going after these accounts could pose a tremendous risk—they were a complete departure from the traditional accounts courted by the bank—there was no business reason not to. In fact, if successful, Jonathan and his bank could "own" this market.

Shortly after he had made his decision to focus on this

niche, his commitment to this direction was tested. "I had called on a CPA who was in charge of a gay street festival. He gave me a proposal: he would switch the festival's entire account over to Wells Fargo if the bank would sponsor the festival and have a presence there," Jonathan recounts. "Going after gay business myself was one thing; to commit the bank to sponsorship of an entire festival was another."

Jonathan decided to go for it. "I had gone this far. If I was going to represent this market, I needed to be totally committed to it," he told us. "To this day I remember writing a memo requesting the bank's presence at the festival and then keeping it in my desk for a week until I gave it my boss."

True to the bank's stated commitment to diversity, Jonathan's boss approved his plan of having the bank sponsor the festival. Although Jonathan was pleased, he still had no idea how successful this would be for the bank. "After all, no bank had ever participated in this festival. That weekend I was really really nervous."

Jonathan's concerns were unfounded. The bank opened a record number of accounts that weekend, and business after business dropped off their cards and asked Jonathan to call on them. "From the start this group was hugely supportive — in part, because Wells Fargo recognized them," he states.

Jonathan had created a niche for himself and for his bank. He began to systematically approach all businesses that had dropped off their cards—and nearly every one of them signed up! Like all successful ventures, the competition was quick to react. Today at the same festival, there are seven banks present trying to court the business that less than ten years ago, no bank wanted. Not only had he branded himself, by electing to stand out by thinking differently and taking a risk, but he created a market for the entire banking industry. See what happens when you brand yourself? Here's what Jonathan's PBS looks like:

Jonathan Weedman's PBS

Jonathan is a progressive and enterprising banking executive not afraid to explore beyond traditional boundaries to help increase the breadth and scope of Wells Fargo's business.

This alone is a branding success story, but is only act one of Jonathan's story. The niche he had created was born out of a business need; he would expand it based on his passion. "When I saw how warmly the gay community had received the bank, I decided to approach the gay-oriented nonprofit organizations as well — organizations such as Project Angel Food (an organization that prepares and delivers meals to AIDS patients) and AIDS Project Los Angeles."

With all the work Jonathan was doing with nonprofit organizations, he suddenly found himself working closely with the Wells Fargo Foundation, the charitable contributions arm of Wells Fargo Bank. Jonathan became very involved with this group and, because of his connection with Gay and Lesbian nonprofit organizations, he found himself the liaison between the bank and these nonprofits. He loved this part of his job, because he felt so strongly about all the good work these nonprofits were doing.

"Wells Fargo is a very smart company that understands the need to target very specific consumer groups. They also knew they had in me, the perfect person to represent the Gay and Lesbian audience," Jonathan says. "With our success with this group, we became identified as the bank of choice for Gays and Lesbians, and a significant amount of business has come our way. We began to be honored by every major and minor Gay and Lesbian group. And I was the logical choice to represent the bank at the galas and charity events where the bank was honored."

So logical, in fact, that the head of the Wells Fargo Foundation called him one day and asked him if he wanted to manage the lower half of the state of California and Arizona for all nonprofit donations. A dream job for Jonathan: "If someone told me that day when I was looking through the Yellow Pages that my decision to go after the gay business niche would lead to being part of the Wells Fargo Foundation team, I wouldn't have believed them. By taking a risk and having the courage to accept the potential downside—while believing in myself, I succeeded far beyond my expectations and I am a happy person for it."

Our next brand profile comes out of the world of publishing.

Standing Out from Her Peers: Judith Regan

You don't have to be in the publishing industry to know Judith's name; currently president of Regan Books, a division of HarperCollins, she makes gossip columns and celebrity reports with the regularity of Gwyneth Paltrow, Sly Stallone, and Sharon Stone. But given her meteoric flight from the position of editor to the top of her industry, it may come as a surprise to hear Judith admit, "I always felt like a fish out of water. Sometimes I knew in my bones that a book had the potential for wild success, but the sales and marketing departments wouldn't share my view. It seemed they were always more concerned with past sales history or what the competition was doing than sticking their necks out to capture the big wave or megatrend. I, on the other hand, didn't care what the competition was up to, because I already knew: they were trying to do exactly what had come out before." Regan continues, "This, by the way, represents the typical 'me-too' corporate mentality, and is a surefire road to average results. Only daring to be different and taking risks results in major success."

Indeed, Judith is someone who practices what she preaches. Her first books at the helm of her eponymous imprint were never less than controversial entries. "But the press and general opinion both got it wrong," she says with a laugh. "Everyone said, 'Oh, yes, Judith Regan. She's the one who does celebrity biographies [the Howard Stern and Rush Limbaugh mammoth hits were hers], and that wasn't it at all. What I did was books that dared to be different, and that is still the basis of my brand, whether the work is a biography, novel, or nonfiction.

"Most people in any industry are too busy looking behind their backs to look forward," Judith continues. "Unlike everybody else, I didn't care what the competition was doing—I cared about what Judith Regan was doing. I wanted my books to dazzle, to be daring, and I still do."

So strong is Judith's brand that we could easily construct her PBS:

Judith Regan's PBS

Judith Regan knows how to spot the megatrends and turn them into blockbuster books by thinking out of the box and following her inner vision and ignoring outer chaos.

Even her catalogs bear the Judith Regan brand. "You should have heard the furor from the sales department the first time my new catalog came out. 'It's too weird, too wild, the books will never sell!' they screamed. Meanwhile," Judith adds with her trademark bravado, "book buyers were asking for extra copies to give to their friends. The traditional publishing catalog is boring and bland; mine is designed like a magazine and makes each book look like a bona fide event. And that, in fact," Judith says, "is my ultimate goal."

Not being afraid to stand out by thinking differently and taking huge risks has paid off for Judith in the corporate world. And although she is, of course, that one-in-a-million individual who can spot trends a mile away, the lessons we can learn from her are immense. Like Jonathan in the previous example, she is not afraid to stand out. She is willing to think differently—in fact, thinking differently is part of her brand—and to take huge risks.

As we counsel people individually about this section of branding, many get a little nervous and begin asking, "But what will my peers think?" Our advice: Don't worry about your peers. Worry about getting your brand noticed. If your way of thinking or the risks you take aren't appreciated, perhaps you have the wrong target audience and you should look elsewhere—in or out of your place of employment or client base—for a different audience who needs what your brand has to offer. Remember, Jonathan and Judith didn't get to where they are by worrying about what others thought. They got to where they are by standing out and letting their brands get noticed.

DON'T TRY TO BE EVERYTHING TO EVERYBODY; INSTEAD, FOCUS ON A SPECIFIC NEED YOUR TARGET AUDIENCE HAS AND THEN DO EVERYTHING YOU CAN TO MEET THAT NEED

We know this sounds simple. It is one of the basic tenets of the book. But it is often overlooked as we move through our careers, so we can't emphasize it enough. Many, many careers were built on this one point. In our experience, most successful managers—no matter at what level—have a strong "number two," that is, someone directly below them who works extremely well with them. They become a team and rely on each other tremendously. That's why it's not unusual for someone to be promoted or move to a different company and take their "number two" with them.

How you become this indispensable is by finding a need that your boss, your division, or your company needs filled and fill it. Let's reexamine how the individuals profiled in this chapter were able to fill unfilled niches:

Name	Niche filled	How their brand allowed them to fill it
Scott James	Provided the president an analysis to prove the profitability of a bonus pack	Strong analytical skills and attention to detail
Jonathan Weedman	Created a new niche the bank could target for additional business	Willingness to risk it all
Judith Regan	Finds and markets new authors and unique concepts	Ability to spot trends and translate them into edgy material

If you look at the niches filled above, they are very specific to the audience our examples are targeting and are based on an individual's skill sets. In other words, each solution is based on their brand.

Now let's examine how Carol Crafton has been able to carve out her brand by providing her target audiences solutions to their specific problems.

Focusing on What the Audiences Need: Carol Crafton

Carol Crafton has a very demanding career as a sales broker; basically, she is a middleman between a manufacturer and the retail stores she is trying to sell to. But not only does she have to keep the manufacturer and retailer happy, she must keep the goals and objectives of her own company in mind as well. It's a difficult balancing act, but Carol has always made herself indispensable to both the manufacturer she represents and the retailer she sells to.

You may be thinking, "How can you possibly brand yourself for two different target audiences that have two different agendas?" It's certainly possible, and no one understands this better than Carol, who has succeeded at her job for years.

Carol confides, "Being a broker is no different than being a mom, and the manufacturer and retailer are the kids. Sometimes they want to play together and sometimes they don't. That's where I come in. Because I do my homework and know both parties so well, I really do know what's best for each of them. And they trust I'll do what is right."

Carol's secret? She has figured out, and focused on, what her audiences need. "At some level the goal of both the retailer and manufacturer—and for that matter, my company as well—is always the same. We all want to make money. My job then becomes simple: How do I best let each of them make money? Because the more money they make, the more money my company makes."

The minute Carol sits down at a meeting, she is prepared and buttoned up on all her facts—about both the retailer's and manufacturer's businesses. Like an expert white-water river-rafting guide, she maneuvers meetings through waters of disagreement to the more sanguine waters of mutual goals. When either the manufacturer or retailer begin to complain, she raises her voice ever so slightly, requesting that all questions be held until after the meeting. But by the time she concludes, there are no questions. She is a master. And her track record proves it. Her business is up 40 percent from a year ago. Neither the manufacturer nor the retailer make a move without her.

"But what about when you have to tell your clients

something they don't want to hear?" we inquired. "It must not be easy to avoid being a 'yes-man' for all your different 'bosses.'"

"The worst thing you can do is not rock the boat," Carol pointed out, "because eventually that boat is going to sink if you don't point out for both parties where it is going. [That's why] being a mom has been the best thing that could have happened to me, both in and out of business. In business, it has taught me to tell the truth, even if the truth wasn't what anyone wanted to hear. Sometimes it is painful, but everyone knows in the long run I am just trying to protect everyone, which is why I have never lost a manufacturer. They trust me and know I'm looking after their best interest—just like a parent does for her child."

Carol Crafton's PBS

Carol is the broker you can trust with your business. With over twenty years' experience without having lost a client, she can find common goals between manufacturer and retailer and always maximize the relationship.

Carol had created a very strong relationship with both manufacturer and retailer by knowing their business, never lying, and always being on the lookout for their mutual objective of making more money. Who wouldn't want someone like this on their team? And who wouldn't want to support her, and give her that promotion?

THE PATH TO SUCCESS

If, in concert with your PBS, you use the three points outlined in this chapter, it's a no-brainer that you'll be creating for yourself, at your company, a dynamic, challenging career with huge, upwardly mobile potential.

As for those of you who want to change careers or are not ensconced in corporate America, the tools to forge your new professional path are in the chapter that follows.

CHAPTER SEVEN

Forging a New Professional Path

In the preceding chapter, we showed how you can use branding to get promoted in the corporate world. Many people we know have done just that, and if we think of individuals who are corporate stars, it's a safe bet to say that all of these folks have brands. On the other hand, we'd be less than honest if we didn't admit that we've all known people who plodded up the corporate ladder, obtaining sequentially higher positions just because they were *there*.

There are two scenarios, however, in which just being there won't work. Here, we're talking about those of you who are:

- changing careers or
- in the process of opening your own small business or private practice.

Either of these career pivots requires much more than just "showing up" at the workplace. Whether you are actively seeking to use your skills in a whole new job area or are starting your own business, an entrepreneurial spirit is absolutely key for achieving the success you deserve.

CHANGING CAREERS

If you're seeking to change fields, branding yourself isn't optional; it's imperative. If you are, for example, a customer service manager with a credit card company who is seeking the exact same job with a new company (whether because you're moving, want to make more money, etc.), branding yourself isn't an absolute must. Certainly, we would always advocate branding yourself as the best customer service manager any firm could wish to hire; if you do, you'll not only get the job you're after, but at the highest possible salary as well. But in the strictest sense, branding isn't de rigueur, because companies hire individuals in like jobs (apples to apples) every day.

But now let's say you're a customer service manager for a credit card company who seeks a job for a customer service manager with a retail furniture establishment. It's possible that a farsighted employer would call you in because you have a similar job in a different field. In today's competitive times, though, it's much more likely that there are more than enough retail customer service managers looking for work that the employer wouldn't have to go outside his industry to find the person he/she wants to hire.

This is why you have to brand yourself—not as a direct marketing (credit card) customer service pro, but as a customer service manager par excellence, one who has the skills and personality that will make you a success in any field of business. (You'll notice that we haven't mentioned the market gap part of the PBS equation, because it's a given here—a job opening does exist, by dint of the newspaper ad.) You are not just a credit card customer service executive, but rather:

A seasoned customer service manager with eight years' experience in all phases of the field, including customer relations, defining corporate policies, and employee training. A results-oriented manager with a B.S. in sales management and three citations for superior performance on the job.

This ups the ante considerably, doesn't it? If you use this PBS as the guiding light of your cover letter and résumé, an interview *will* ensue. Rather than saying, "This person has no retail customer service experience," the hiring authority is going to say, "Wow—what a winner! This individual's got all the goods, and citations to prove it." Your goal, of course, should be not merely to be called in for an interview, but to dare the prospective employer *not* to see you for fear of losing someone of your background, professional "can-do" attitude, and skill. In a sense, this is what Norah Lawlor did beautifully.

Making Herself the Winning Candidate: Norah Lawlor

We ran into publicist, writer, and woman-about-town Norah Lawlor one night at a soirée for the ultrachic hotel consortium, the Leading Hotels of the World, at New York's tony Pierre hotel. "Norah!" we exclaimed. "Once again we meet! We seem to see you out wherever we go."

We were momentarily confused when Norah laughed heartily. "That's so funny," she exclaimed, "and that's precisely my strategy. I'm so glad you finally caught on!"

"Come again?" we begged.

"Do you have a minute?" she asked. "Let's park ourselves by the seafood table, and I'll tell you a little story."

We went with Norah at once; her stories, usually involving the celeb *du moment*, are even more delicious than the shrimp. This time, however, the tale was about herself.

"Forgive me if I beam," she said. "But I just won a fabulous account: the Plaza Athenée [one of America's most elegant hotels]. And let me tell you how. When I met with the hotel's general manager, he said, 'I know you. I've seen you everywhere!'—and indeed he had. You see, I make it my business to *be* everywhere I can in the upscale market: at functions and parties in New York, Palm Beach, abroad, wherever. That's because upmarket properties want one of their own—or someone they perceive as their own—to represent them to the press. If I stayed at home every night watching sitcoms, I wouldn't have a single account."

"Congrats, Norah. You're busier than anyone we know. But we always thought you represented only restaurants and clubs."

Once again our friend laughed. "We are what we think we are," Norah advised. "If I'd never sought to reinvent myself, I'd still be back in Ottawa, doing God knows what. No, I decided I wanted to expand my business to the area of hotels and resorts, and knew my background as a publicist in the restaurant and nightlife field would serve me well. Except for one thing: I'd never actually represented a hotel. So I had to be *perceived* as a hotel publicist—and again, this would never have happened if I'd chosen to stay home watching *Friends*. It was incumbent upon me to make my face known—at the resorts and, more important, at hotel industry functions like the one we're attending now. Get it?"

Indeed we do! Norah is powerful proof that living your brand is the best way to make it—and you—known. She set her sights, defined her brand, and made it happen.

But let's be honest here: a new brand alone can not take you into an entirely new field without changing the skills part of your PBS. It's essential that you know and have the minimum requirements for entry in your chosen field—*then* you can brand yourself for career success! For instance, you can't become a lawyer without going to law school and passing the bar, just as you can't work as a teacher without being certified by the state. However, restating your brand *can* help you segue into a new area or career sector when your skills and experience are actually applicable to your goal.

Finding a New Job in a Similar Field: Alice Andrews

When we first met Alice, she was a public relations manager for a consortium representing food products made in Italy and distributed in the United States and Canada. To many people, Alice had a dream job: she traveled extensively, wined and dined the press, and hosted press events all across North America. There was just one problem: none of the above was what Alice really wanted to do.

Even the most cursory application of our BAT would have revealed that fact. Alice certainly had the skills to do her job, but being in publicity reflected neither her personality nor her passion. Fact is, although she was fluent in Italian, loved that country, and was a real "foodie" who had contributed articles to several gourmet magazines, dealing with the press wasn't her bailiwick. Alice is a rather reserved woman who feels more comfortable in front of her word processor than in front of a roomful of people. Her friends just couldn't understand why she was so unhappy—and so unfulfilled—in what appeared to be a "glamour job."

Which led us to ask Alice why she was still banging her head against the wall in public relations. Why wasn't she editing a food and wine magazine, or working as a cookbook editor at a major publishing house?"

When we made this suggestion, Alice looked at us, half-wondrous and half-bemused. "Could I really do that?" she nearly gasped out loud.

"But of course you could!" we responded. "You've studied cooking at the Cordon Bleu in Paris. You've contributed articles on food and wine to many national publications. You have a degree from a great college, plus contacts in the food world galore. Who better than you to work as a food editor, either at a magazine or publishing firm?"

Still Alice resisted. "But I've never done that before."

Alice was being shortsighted. "Alice," Rick explained, "nobody is born a food editor, or a baseball player, or the president of the United States. We make ourselves so. And with your background, you can segue into this new field just by crafting a new PBS and making it the focal point of your job campaign."

With a bit more prodding, Alice saw the light . . . especially after we formulated the following PBS for her:

> A food and wine expert who has contributed to *Gourmet*, *Food & Wine*, the *New York Times*, and many other publications. A Wellesley graduate with substantial publicity and administrative experience in the gourmet field who is also a Cordon Bleu–trained chef.

Quite a résumé, wouldn't you say? So what if Alice hadn't been an editor *per se*; plenty of magazine and book companies would jump at the chance to interview such a well-rounded, passionate gourmet enthusiast for an editorial opening. And so they did: Alice now works as an editor of a major food publication that is distributed nationwide.

Why did Alice succeed—and why will *you*? By answering the following questions before crafting your new PBS:

- Why am I different from everyone else?
- Are my true passions and personality reflected here?
- Am I making the most of my education, job training, and skills; and are they stated in my cover letter and résumé?

Most important of all:

- What is my brand?

Another word of advice is important here. Many folks, be it due to downsizing, the elimination of lifetime employment, personal dissatisfaction, or a host of other factors, are searching for a new job field. Unfortunately, many do so as if they were grasping for straws. Granted, it is not an easy process, especially if they are having difficulty trying to pay for food and rent.

If you are in this predicament, or if you are merely seeking to locate a new job field, you should do the following:

- *Consider your personality/passions and skills that you delineated as part of your Brand Assessment Test.* This is where you will find the goods that will guide you to a change in career.

For example, if Alice hadn't had us as career coaches, she could just have easily directed herself toward the editing field. Her passions would have listed gourmet food, books, and cooking, and her skills would have indicated writing and languages. Many of you also may have thought that Alice ought to have pursued a freelance writing career. Yes, Alice is certainly capable enough, but this is where her personality came into play: as we said before, Alice is more timid than go-getting, and so she just doesn't have the personality to deal with the constant rejection all writers face. Thus, the rather more stable job of an editor suits her personality, as well as her skills.

So, too, should you consider your *skills* as well as personality/passion in targeting a new career goal, and let them direct your aspirations. For example, if you are a lawyer, don't start thinking about becoming an astronaut; instead, think about new places and/or ways in which you could practice law. (Fact is, if you're really interested in aerospace, why not become a practicing attorney at NASA or Boeing?) Look at the ways, means, and places in which your trade or profession are practiced—or, slightly further afield, industries or practices allied to it—to find new positions that are right for you.

• *Look for gaps in the market that you can fill.* By this, we mean both jobs that your skills can fill and expanding industries where your passions and skills can be applied. It is important to be realistic as to economic conditions as well as your own background, training, and skill set.

Let's look at the example of Tom Iorio. Tom graduated from college with a degree in economics, then spent several years in China working for financial institutions. When he returned to New York, he knew the life of an economist or banker was not for him, and that computer applications were the passion he wanted to pursue.

But although he was familiar with several programs and semiversant in a few more, Tom recognized that he had to develop and hone his skills. "Most of all, I wanted some hands-on experience in companies using computer programs for economic models and multimedia design. Plus, I needed to support myself, so working as a temp with my existing skills made more sense than going back to school, especially because I wasn't sure exactly what I wanted to do," he notes.

After getting settled in Manhattan, Tom made the rounds of the temp agencies, registering with every one requiring specialized computer knowledge. "I wasn't the computer whiz of all time, but I certainly could do more than just word processing. The most important thing is that, at each job, I made it my business to learn every computer program I could when there was downtime. In fact, this is something I can't recommend highly enough. While most of my coworkers spent their free time talking on the phone to friends, I used tutorials to learn programs I'd never even seen before."

It was a plan that worked like a charm. "I started out making fourteen dollars an hour; then sixteen dollars, eighteen dollars, and was earning thirty dollars an hour at the end of my temp tenure because of all the specialized programs I knew. It doesn't matter what your field is or what kind of company you're working in," Tom says, "never stop amassing new skills. It's the surest path to long-term success, not to mention a fulfilling workday in the short term."

Like Tom, we also believe in pragmatism, not pipe dreams. Tom had an idea of what he wanted to do, but he knew he lacked the skills. Well, he got them, but he also got something else: a newfound knowledge of gaps in the market. For while still a temp, Tom kept his eyes open. "Just because you're working on a temporary basis doesn't mean you're any less a part of a company's workforce," Tom believes. And he used temping as a terrific opportunity to scout out the market and identify emerging trends, both in his immediate environment and in his field as a whole.

As Tom recalls, "I saw the banking industry changing practically in front of my eyes, in that the function of computers in producing graphics for client presentations was of ever greater importance. For the first time, print shops were becoming obsolete, as you could custom design a presentation for clients on an individual basis. Yet there was no continuity within banks' computer departments, which were nothing more than a couple of managers and a constantly changing stream of temps."

What Tom did is what all superior self-branders did: he identified a market niche and filled it. "Not only did I have excellent computer skills by now, but I was an economics major at Columbia with professional experience in the field. How's that for a great brand?" he asks, and who among us could help but agree?

"I established The Rio Group as a one-stop shop for computer graphics in the banking industry. What we offered that no one else did was a pool of talented labor; complete confidentiality; and, more important than anything, the ability to take projects off our clients' hands and return gorgeous presentations with a modicum of input and investment of their time. Top-drawer firms prefer to maintain long-term relationships with suppliers they can trust, rather than reinventing the wheel each time a new temp comes on board for three weeks. Rio is actually much cheaper [for banks] in the long run because of this lack of overhead, plus we provide the best service and product in the field."

Tom's story of being a successful, savvy self-brander who took stock of the economic environment before selecting his exact job target leads us directly into the next section—on how to open the small business of your dreams.

OPENING THE SMALL BUSINESS OR PRIVATE PRACTICE OF YOUR DREAMS

According to conventional wisdom, most start-up businesses or consultancies fail due to one overriding reason: lack of funds. It is true that a certain amount of money is required for some start-ups, such as retail establishments or businesses that require substantial technical equipment (a dentist's office or computer concern, for instance).

However, we believe that it is not a lack of funds, but

of strategic positioning, that most often explains the early demise of business ventures of all kinds. (In addition, poor management skills also can explain why new businesses fail.) And of all the strategies and tactics you set forth for your small business or private practice, a branding statement is the most important of all. So unless you have a lot of luck, world-class contacts, or a Bill Gates–sized trust fund, you'd better forge a winning PBS before taking the plunge.

Why is a branding statement so important when you open your own business, consultancy, or private practice? Because, just as when you seek a new job, career change, or promotion, you need to be able to state clearly and unequivocally why you are better than the rest, and what service(s) you offer that set you ahead of the pack.

In fact, we believe that there is no career sector in which branding yourself is more important than when you are in business for yourself. This is because, unless you're a trust-fund darling or have a rich spouse, the receipts of your business—your very lifeline—are dependent on you and you alone. Look at it this way:

• If you are a chiropractor affiliated with an HMO, a certain amount of business will come your way as a matter of course. You could certainly brand yourself to become the most requested chiropractor in your service provider area or to gain promotions or key assignments, but you would still make a certain amount of money regardless of whether you branded yourself or not.

• If, on the other hand, you are a chiropractor in business for yourself, a PBS is key. It is entirely up to you to have a winning Personal Branding Statement to use in your publicity materials, your brochures, and in your conversations with patients, so that they will keep coming back to your office and refer their friends and family to you.

But how do you go about developing your own new business successfully? Remember your skills, remember your passions—and read the following case histories to find out!

Succeeding with a New Business: Wolfgang Wind

Wolfgang was an Austrian national working as a successful building contractor in Los Angeles when the recession of the early '90s hit all of southern California hard. Suddenly home prices nose-dived and new building came to a standstill—this, coupled with overbuilding during the previous few years, meant the local construction industry was at an all-time low. Wolfgang couldn't afford to languish, so he did what anyone seeking to brand themselves to change careers should do: he took pen to paper and made a list of personal and professional skills that might lead him to a new career.

When you do this yourself, remember the directive of day one of your Brand Assessment Test: Let your mind run wild, but do think in terms of concrete affinities, achievements, and skills. If you didn't finish high school, don't write down "Become a brain surgeon" unless you want to spend more than a decade in school, internship, and residency. In fact, you shouldn't feel compelled to put down any concrete career at all. This is not about listing job titles, but about delineating those skills and qualities that will help you define a new professional role.

In Wolfgang's case, he came up with following list:

- speak German
- know some film stars
- have personal connections that can lead me to other stars
- was a marketing director in Europe
- have family and other connections to important people in Austria

- know people in European press
- like to ski
- was junior European windsurfing champion
- don't want nine-to-five office job
- would like to be able to travel to Europe

Wolfgang wasn't afraid to list his personal passions along with his professional strengths. Whether he actually incorporated them into a new career goal or branding statement remained to be seen, but putting these thoughts to paper in the order in which they came to him helped him determine which aspects of his working and personal life were really the most important to him.

The list complete, Wolfgang began to mull over the possibilities. The first thought that came to him—after all, he was working in L.A., the quintessential one-industry town—was to somehow work in publicity or marketing for a movie studio in Hollywood. He followed up by calling friends in the business and meeting executive recruiters in the Los Angeles area. The consensus was clear (if dismaying): already in his thirties and without directly related corporate experience, Wolfgang could hardly jump on board as a film industry publicity executive.

Wolfgang reminded himself of the two questions "What do I have to offer that no one else can?" and "What can I do better than anyone else?" and began reevaluating his possibilities. What he had to do, he figured after several weeks' time, was offer a product no one else could, and brand himself as the person to fulfill that role. After brainstorming for hours on end, Wolfgang figured that he could use his language skills and knowledge of the foreign press to fulfill one important role: to devise and implement promotions geared at gaining Hollywood stars and their movies space in the European, specifically German-speaking, press.

But how would he start? It was no use coming up with a corporate or even Personal Branding Statement till he had a finite idea of precisely what Transcontinental Publicity and Promotions—the brand name of what would be his new company came easily to him, and it fulfilled all the requirements cited on pages 110–111—could do. So Wolfgang referred to his list, and his eyes kept going back to the word *ski*. "Wouldn't it be great," he mused, "if I could somehow combine a public relations business with time on the slopes?"

Eureka! "Well, why not?" Wolfgang thought. "The Austrian Alps are so beautiful that even the most jaded Hollywood stars couldn't pass up a trip to visit, especially those who are known skiers. Perhaps I could organize some kind of a publicity event there. If the celebrities got first-class air tickets and five-star hotels, even the biggest names would be happy to come." But to what? "It couldn't be an obvious publicity stunt; the press can smell a rat a mile away. It would," Wolfgang thought, "have to be something beneficial, humanitarian . . . a charity event!" he deduced, nearly leaping out of his chair. "What could be better than that?"

Having deduced this unique market position, Wolfgang was ready to take a stab at creating his Personal Branding Statement. This is the one he devised:

> A seasoned marketing and publicity professional with extensive experience in planning promotional events in Europe, with an eye on garnering maximum European exposure for Hollywood projects and personalities. An Austrian native whose goal is obtaining one-of-a-kind coverage in the foreign press.

Wow! Wolfgang etched out a Personal Branding Statement that met every self-brander's two main goals: (1) It provided a cogent, concise overview of his unique set of strengths, and (2) It told why he can do it better than anyone else. It doesn't matter whether you're working with Hollywood stars or crunching numbers for an actuarial firm. Whoever you are, wherever you may be, you can brand yourself to be the best in your new field.

Now here's an example of an entrepreneur who used his *job skills* to identify a gap in the marketplace and start a booming business.

Succeeding with a New Business: Mike Beer

Mike was an extremely successful real estate executive who specialized in buying foreclosed properties. Many of these, he came to realize, were luxury hotels that had not properly marketed themselves or suffered from excessive competition in their local markets, thus forcing them into bankruptcy and foreclosure.

"What a shame," Mike thought, "that such gorgeous properties should fail; some were even landmarks of historical interest. There's got to be some way to save these hotels and preserve these treasured pieces of architecture." The answer wasn't obscure or arcane. All it would take, Mike realized, was increasing the occupancy rate so that the hotels could stay afloat. Since these were great places to stay, he reasoned, the lack of revenue must derive from a real or imagined perception that these luxury hotels' rates were too high.

So why not offer these world-class hotel rooms at lower rates? It would certainly be better than keeping them empty due to room tariffs that were sky-high. Thus Room Exchange was born. Mike Beer noted a market need, used a common-sense approach to filling it, and initiated a company devoted to buying blocks of luxury rooms at a discount, then offering these to consumers at rates 35 to 70 percent off published rates.

More than merely starting a company, Mike actually created an industry—one stemming not from a pie-in-the-sky idea but from the realities of the area in which he already worked. Today, Room Exchange holds rooms at twenty-three thousand hotels around the world, and has been hailed by the media from coast to coast.

See? It doesn't take an M.B.A. to deduce brilliant new brands—just a knowledge of one's own profession, an open mind, and, when necessary, a drive to acquire the new skills and training required to succeed.

A FEW LAST WORDS OF ADVICE

Carving out an identity for an entirely new career isn't child's play; neither is crafting the business or private practice of your dreams. But remember you're *not* pulling your brand out of thin air, even when you're devising an entirely new field or business. The completion of the Brand Assessment Test ensures that you are using hard data, not mere dreams or hopes, to review your skills and accomplishments, consider your passions and personality type, then learn the market conditions as a means of developing a brand.

Nowhere is this equation more valid, more necessary, than when you're seeking to forge entirely new professional paths. Which is why we want you to think long and hard about the following piece of advice: *Whether you're looking to brand yourself to further your existing career or to develop an entirely new one, always begin your quest in your own professional backyard. The grass may seem greener elsewhere, but the most fertile fields grow close to home.*

Yes, belief in oneself can work wonders like nothing else can. But goals are just pipe dreams without the knowledge and elbow grease required to get there.

CHAPTER EIGHT

Jump-Starting Stalled Brands

As you read this, you will already have crafted your own brand statement, and begun to present to the world the new and improved you.

Unfortunately, the calls and letters aren't flooding in, and it is becoming apparent that the branding statement you have crafted is not making quite the impact you had expected. Don't panic: all your work has not been for naught. Instead, it is just a case of needing to fine-tune one or more elements of your PBS to come up with a more winning brand.

How do you do this? By examining each part of your brand statement, one by one, to see what adjustments need to be made. In the following examples, we show you the major, but easily repairable, problems of recently crafted brands and then suggest how to rethink each brand element to make sure that your brand wins in the marketplace.

ARE ALL THE ELEMENTS OF MY BRAND WORKING TOGETHER HARMONIOUSLY?

"Oftentimes when a new brand is placed on the market and there doesn't appear to be immediate acceptance, it's because one of the marketing elements is slightly off," says Stu Fine, senior vice president of marketing at Alberto-Culver (and former new products brand manager for that firm). "The packaging may be the wrong color. The price may be too high or low. All are easily fixable problems. The point is, before you shut the brand down, you should carefully evaluate all your marketing elements piece by piece."

Excellent advice! Never beat a hasty retreat from your carefully crafted brand, or disband it until you've reviewed all its elements. Chances are you'll discover it's a perfectly valid positioning, and one or two of its aspects require clarification or retooling. Or, its marketing may be slightly off. All you may need to do is fine-tune the broadcasting of your brand.

The first questions to consider are these:

• Is your résumé, or business brochure, reflective of your brand character, and does it clearly state its unique benefits?

• Are you broadcasting your brand to the right audience? You can have the best brand in the world, but unless your target is dead-on accurate, you won't enjoy optimal success.

• Is the personal package correct (i.e., Are your clothing, hair, and style right for the targets you've chosen)?

• Is your company or practice packaged correctly? Re-evaluate your office, marketing materials, and other elements before broadcasting them.

We realize that it's difficult to critique one's own work, so this is where one-on-one focus groups can be useful. After all, the world's largest multinational marketing companies use focus groups to test new products time and time again; doesn't your newly developed brand merit the same troubleshooting tool?

Here's a story that proves our point. We had lunch one

day with our former client, Karla Kaufman. Karla is a television producer who spent years in the trenches of tabloid TV gaining valuable contacts and skills. We had structured her combination of talents—always considering her personality and passions—into this brand statement:

> No producer has the ability to turn a story around quicker than Karla Kaufman. Known for two-hour turnaround on stories that would take other producers two days, Karla is the one to rely on when time is tight. With her effervescent personality and natural sense of comedy, she's the producer every reporter and cameraperson wants to work with—even if a story takes all night.

At lunch, Karla told us of a recent incident where all the elements of her brand statement weren't coming together just right: "I had taken a job based solely on the skill part of my brand statement. The executive producer needed someone who could turn a story around immediately, and I knew I could do that," Karla shared.

"But about a week into the job, I was miserable. Not because of lack of skills, but because something was missing for me. It wasn't until about a week later that I could finally put my finger on it, and as I reviewed my PBS—you guys are right to advise people to do that on an almost daily basis—I knew exactly what it was. No one on this show's staff had a sense of humor, or frankly, any discernible personality at all. Every time I tried to crack a joke or be funny," Karla related, "I was met with odd stares. Suddenly I realized I wasn't being true to myself or my brand."

Shortly after coming to this realization, Karla went to the show's executive producer and tendered her resignation. A few days later she found another producing job on a program whose chief not only appreciated her skill but her nifty personality as well. As of this writing, Karla is still having a blast!

You, too, should be honest with yourself, both about your overall PBS and each element it contains. If, after evaluation, you're stumped as to your brand's problem, it wouldn't hurt to go back and do another round of one-on-one interviews. After all, marketers—and the most successful self-branders—do it all the time.

AM I TARGETING THE RIGHT AUDIENCE?

If you are in business for yourself and are targeting new customers, you need to know who and what they are. Let's say you're a dry cleaner who wants to open a store in a new neighborhood. It's important—no, absolutely *vital*—that you know who the people living in that part of town are, both demographically and psychographically. (That is, how much money they have and what their attitudes and preferences are.) If you are opening in an affluent city or neighborhood, price may be less important than a beautiful storefront and interior, and you may need special machinery or employee training to clean silk, fancy leather, and fur. If, on the other hand, you see the need for a dry cleaner in a working-class town or poor, modest urban neighborhood, then price is going to be key. And the only way you can know this is to know who your customers are.

Endré, one of our clients, was looking to establish a niche fitness business. His plan was to target a high-end clientele who would pay for his combined nutrition and training expertise. Once his brand was stated, he began the marketing of *brand Endré*.

Our client had beautiful brochures printed up with his

Herculean profile boldly and beautifully positioned on the front cover. Inside, he carefully laid out his services, which included home training, design and implementation of a personal nutrition plan, and ongoing progress monitoring. (The latter was an integral part of his brand, and an area in which most of his competition fell down.) Endré was a tad pricey, but he knew that there was no dearth of ultrarich prospective customers in Hollywoodland.

Endré then bought a mailing list to which he could send his brochures. Once they were in the mail, he waited for the phone to ring. It didn't. In panic mode, the one in which many new brand managers find themselves, Endré phoned us to ask what was wrong.

After reviewing and analyzing all he had done, we, too, were momentarily stumped. Until David asked to see his mailing list. When asked where he had obtained it, Endré told us it was from a friend who promoted nightclubs in L.A. Immediately two facts became apparent: (1) the zip codes of most of the addresses were not in the more affluent parts of town; and (2) most of the people on the list were college students, nightlife denizens, and newly minted yuppies whose BMW payments hardly left them with the cash to afford an expensive private trainer/nutritionist.

In sum, Endré had all the right marketing ingredients but the wrong target audience. We quickly fixed this faux pas by nabbing a new mailing list focusing on the most upscale parts of L.A. Beverly Hills 90210? You bet!

The same kind of thinking holds true if you are targeting companies, large or small. Sandra, a bookkeeper, targets small businesses like clothing shops and restaurants as clients. She needs to know not only how they operate, but what they are looking for in a freelance bookkeeper. By knowing this, she is able to work their preferences directly into her own brand statement.

Similarly, when we authors do marketing consulting work for a company we've never worked for before, we can't go in blind. (Or we could, but we probably wouldn't get much work.) Instead, we need to know as much as we can about these companies and what they do—information gleaned from the newspaper, business journals, and personal contacts—so that we can pitch ourselves with optimal results.

So remember that it's quite possible that there's nothing at all wrong with your brand, but it's simply that you're not broadcasting it to the right audience. Reevaluate your targets, be they consumers or your boss. Do they really need the benefits of your brand? If not, there is almost certainly another target audience that would be receptive to the brand benefits you provide.

DOES MY BRAND TRULY PROVIDE A UNIQUE AND MEANINGFUL BENEFIT?

More product brands fail because they don't provide a consumer meaningful benefits than for any other reason. It seems logical that this is the selfsame explanation of why our professional brands don't succeed as well as we would like.

Go back to your own brand statement. Is your benefit truly unique? To stand out among the crowd in a competitive market, it must. Again, use focus groups; it's helpful to poll colleagues and, better still, prospective clients who use people in your field. What about your brand statement could be better, tighter, more exclusive, and make your targets feel they'd be crazy to not consider using you?

In the course of our consulting work, we often find clients who don't want to take the time or exert enough thought in exploring the brand benefits of their PBS to the fullest possible extent.

Our client, Gena, was a perfect example of this. Gena was a highly talented interior designer who was more anxious to serve her clients' needs than her own. Rather than really diving in and uncovering her unique, consumer-meaningful skills and traits, Gena hurriedly put together a brand statement at one of our seminars, and ran out the door before the session was done, thinking that was the last she'd see of us.

Several weeks later, Gena called and asked sheepishly if we would help her refine her statement. She admitted it had been put together in haste and wasn't working at all. We asked her to fax her statement, which read:

> Gena has a knack for interior design, whether it is for private or professional clients. Easy to work with and always amenable to clients' suggestions, Gena will get the job done right and on time.

Her target audience? The ill-defined "anyone who needs the inside of their house or business designed." Talk about generic! As we broke down this brand statement, we asked ourselves the following questions:

- Is there a skill? (Answer: Yes, "a knack for interior design.")
- Are there distinct personality traits? (Answer: Gena is easy to work with and open to suggestions.)
- Is there a target audience? (Answer: Yes, anyone looking for an interior designer.)

So if all the components are in place, what precisely is wrong with her PBS? Let's count it up: First, Gena's skill is utterly generic; and, as banal and undefined as it is, she still hasn't provided the proof to back up her statement. Second, the target is too broad. She might as well have said, "the whole human race." Third, because the target is not refined, there's no way possible she can broadcast her brand.

We scheduled a session with Gena to delve more deeply into her skill set. We discovered she had worked for several nationally recognized interior designers all through college. After graduating, she worked with a distinguished architectural firm. By the time she was twenty-six, gifted Gena had almost ten years' elite professional experience behind her! Further, we found out that she much preferred designing industrial spaces to private homes, and in fact, that is where the bulk of her experience lay. Finally, we learned that Gena had highly specific training in modern design and in the development and use of textures and materials.

Because Gena needed special help, we conducted a one-on-one with several of her former bosses. What we found was that Gena had a natural ability to mix and match unusual textures, patterns, and other elements, and in fact designed several new ones herself. What we learned from Gena herself was that she was a mom who wanted to work from home while she was raising her young children. Time with them was terribly important to her, yet she didn't want to abandon her hard-won professional role completely.

With this new information in our arsenal, we set out to create a brand statement that was as unique as Gena herself:

> Gena's ten years of experience working closely with national design leaders has made her an expert in modern interior design. Her acclaimed ability to mix unusual textures and patterns makes her a designer not of the ordinary, but of distinction. Realizing that time is of the essence, she completes projects on schedule and with cost-efficiency.

It follows naturally that Gena's target audience is businesses interested in preemptive modern interior design.

Two statements, same person, same skill sets, and same personality; but one is as different from the other as night is from day. What makes the second one so much stronger? It captures who Gena is and what she is all about . . . what makes her unique. To work optimally, your brand statement should do exactly the same.

CAN I REALLY DELIVER ON MY BRAND PROMISE?

Consumers hate to be deceived, and potential bosses and clients are no different. An altogether too common branding problem is overpromising on one or more advertised benefits. Just as consumers may buy a brand once but won't do so twice if the product doesn't deliver, so, too, will a potential client of yours. A much better strategy is to isolate what you really do well, rather than trying to impress people with things you can only do averagely.

One of our clients, for instance, asked us for help in achieving his goal: obtaining the vice presidency of a major bank. However, as we began the process of researching the skills required for this job and comparing them to his own skill set, we quickly saw there was no way to get him from point A to point B; his skill set did not equip him adequately for the job.

Be honest about your skill sets so that disappointment won't ensue. If there is a goal that you really want to reach, then set yourself a plan of attack, and go about obtaining the proper skill sets that will bring you within reach of your goal.

Author David Andrusia made this mistake once—but only once. As a freelance copywriter, he pitched his way into an assignment for a highly technical electronics brochure. The pay was great, which is why he wanted the job so badly, but he soon discovered he was in way over his head. David was summarily fired from this project because although he had formulated a wonderful brand, he lacked the skill set to back it up. This is why it's critical that you deliver on *all* of the promises of your brand statement.

IS MY PRIME BENEFIT REALLY SOMETHING THE MARKET NEEDS?

Amazing brand benefits are all well and good, but if it's not something the market needs, you won't be successful. The grocery world is full of examples of new products that companies thought were brilliant—remember New Coke?—but that nobody wanted to have. By the same token, you may have a wonderfully unique brand component, such as fluency in Swahili, but unless you're planning to open up new markets in Africa, it isn't of much benefit to your prospective boss.

Again here's an example from our personal archives. When he was a marketing executive at Revlon, David (who was a French major in college) sought to move into the company's international division. While interviewing, he put the primary focus on his foreign-language prowess. That's a lovely skill, of course, but David failed to adequately research his target's needs. (Remember that the target can be either your present employer, a new company, or clients if you're a freelancer/consultant.) After interviewing unsuccessfully for several international slots, he did some sleuthing and discovered a vital point he had overlooked: because most European executives speak good to excellent English, the foreign-language ability of American executives was not considered a major asset by the international division's hiring authorities. Nor, interestingly, was product development talent (highly important to domestic cosmetics marketers).

Rather, what the international group sought was a sales promotion background, since marketing personnel were promoting existing products, not creating new ones. Had he done his homework and realized what his target audience was looking for, David would have done himself a great service—and probably gotten the international job he sought for so long.

Business owners and freelancers can fall into this trap, too. Ever wonder why seemingly charming or much-needed shops open and close in months flat? Typically it's because of a bad match between merchandise (or food or services provided) and the neighborhood. Several years ago, on the Greenwich Village–East Village border, a well-designed hair salon catering to African Americans opened up. Specializing in braids and extensions, the owners capitalized on a bona fide market gap: the lack of upscale salons for black hair. Moreover, they had struck an excellent balance between stuffy "uptown" places and too-trendy "downtown" shops.

Thus, the market gap they had discerned was a strong one. But in answering the question, "Is my prime benefit really something the market needs?" they failed to adequately address the full ramifications of the word *market*. Yes, a market for their shop existed, but not in the location they chose: the neighborhood just didn't have many black residents, and the shop was not on a busy commercial street where people from all over New York come to shop.

You can avoid making the same mistake by understanding that *market* is defined not only in a larger, macroeconomic sense, but in the more commonplace definition of the word as a neighborhood or environs. Offering a senior citizens' discount for hairstyling is a great idea if you're near a retirement community, but not in a hip, young community; similarly, fancy, high-priced food items will do well in Bethesda or Beverly Hills, but not in a neighborhood that's working class. Match your benefits to the market for surefire success;

mismatch, and you'll miss the job or customer you might otherwise easily have had.

IS MY BRAND MISSING A KEY ELEMENT?

Sometimes there is nothing wrong with the brand or brand strategy, but a marketing element is missing. The classic example here is Crest toothpaste. A pioneer in the use of fluoride, Crest was an excellent product, but by no means the toothpaste category leader when it was introduced. Something was missing in the marketing mix, something that would convince consumers just how good this product was.

It wasn't until Crest received an outside endorsement from the American Dental Association (ADA) that the product took off, eventually becoming one of the most well known brands of all time. Reconsider your brand to see if there isn't one added element that will differentiate it from the competition. (Your focus group members may well help you here.) For instance, ten years ago a graphic artist who worked on a computer was big news. Today, drawing boards are virtually obsolete, and a designer who truly wants to prove himself head and shoulders above the rest needs to advertise that he knows new programs, works in multimedia, or has other technological wizardry that puts him ahead of the pack.

IS MY BRAND TOO BROAD?

You can't please all the people all the time, and a brand is no different. Many highly promoted brands have failed because they were marketed to the entire world, not to one or more well-defined market segments. Similarly, whether you're after a corporate job or are self-employed, you need to know exactly what kinds of companies to target or who your main client base will be. In general, it's best to keep to one or two strongly defined benefits and drive 'em all the way home.

For example, one of our clients, Steve, had recently received a master's degree in social research and was hunting for a job. This newly minted researcher wanted to do it all, but he found out the hard way that an overly broad brand is almost as bad as having no brand at all. In interview after interview, Steve was asked what type of research he did best. Invariably he would answer, "I can conduct any kind of research you want me to," and leave it at that. He also always left without the job.

As his list of target organizations got shorter and shorter, Steve came to us for help. First, we scanned his résumé. It was certainly impressive, but, like the people who had interviewed him, we came to the same conclusion: an objective of "research" or calling oneself a researcher is far too broad a base. Steve had to specify an area, preferably one representing a unique market niche.

"If you had to pick one area of research, what would it be?" we asked.

"I'd be out in the field interviewing people and coming to conclusions based on their points of view," Steve replied.

Now we were getting somewhere!

"And what subjects do you most like to explore?" we continued.

"Religion. Social issues," he replied.

The bull's-eye was now in sight!

"And what makes you a great researcher—better than anyone else?" we finally asked.

"Why, I can take seemingly unconnected bits and pieces of people's interviews and connect them in a quantifiable and coherent fashion," Steve said with confidence.

Superb. We now had the makings of a meaningful brand statement.

Interviewing people in order to understand their attitudes on religious and social issues, assembling this into quantifiable data, then drawing conclusions is Steve's specialty. According to his professors, "Steve not only collects magnificent data but analyzes it better than anyone else in his class."

However, when we showed this brand statement to Steve, he was obviously annoyed. "What's the problem?" we asked.

"This is too narrow a target!" he moaned. "I'll never get a job. Who wants a 'religious researcher'?"

Patiently, we asked Steve to at least try this brand on for size. After all, his old way of looking for a job wasn't working. What did he have to lose? In addition, instead of waiting for interviewers to come to campus—a purely passive mode—we recommended that he compile a target list and go straight to the organizations for which he most wanted to work. Again, research on your target market is not an extra added attraction but the main event.

Talk about a sea change! Within a month Steve landed two job offers: one from the headquarters of a national religious organization and another from a university doing social research. By defining his brand, Steve was able to match his unique skills to the needs of prospective employers and tell them exactly what he could do for them. And that's where branding works best of all: it allows you to target jobs based on your personality and skills—and get them.

AM I LIVING MY BRAND?

One of our clients called us about two weeks after we had developed what we thought was a superior branding statement for him. He was noticeably irritated. When we asked specifically what the problem was, he shot back, "This brand thing is the problem. It's not working at all."

"What's not working?" we asked.

"No one sees a change; no one even knows I *have* a brand!" he practically yelled into the phone.

"Well, let's talk about this," we offered, trying to calm him down. "Let's start at the beginning: What's your branding statement?"

"Er, um, I don't have it on the tip of my tongue. Repeating my branding statement isn't the only thing I do all day," he snapped. "I have to go to my desk to find it," he added, sputtering.

We knew what the problem was at once. Your PBS is not a pretty accessory, some auxiliary part of your life. If you don't make your branding statement part of you, it is not going to work. It should be considered a living, breathing document that is meant to be with you constantly—your professional lungs, if you like. Pin it to your mirror and read it as an affirmation every morning. Tuck it into your purse or wallet and pull it out to read several times during the day.

Ultimately, you should become so familiar with your statement that you can rattle it off anytime, anywhere. Make it part of your conscious and subconscious mind; make it part of you! Do this, and we promise success through branding will be yours.

WHEN EVERYTHING'S RIGHT, BUT NOTHING IS WORKING: RESTAGING A BRAND

Sometimes, even after extensive testing of concept and positioning, and when all elements of the branding statement appear to be in place, a brand does not work once it is thrust into the marketplace. This, too, can happen with our career brands (even if rarely).

The classic restaging story in product development involves a woman-targeted cigarette that just didn't seem to catch on. Having invested heavily in this new brand, the manufacturers were concerned. Should they pull the product from the market altogether? At the last minute, the advertising agency stepped in and asked if they could take a second look at the brand. After careful evaluation, they realized the market didn't need another women's cigarette. What they suggested made the manufacturer very nervous. The agency recommended focusing on an image of a person who was to embody the character of the cigarette: not a woman, but a macho man. Desperate and out of ideas, the manufacturer hesitatingly agreed ... then held its collective breath. Accordingly, the brand had a new image, new advertising, and a new package look. (Keep in mind that the product itself hadn't changed one bit; the branding, however, had made a 180-degree turn.) What the agency had done was to restage Marlboro, now one of the world's most viable, visible, and valuable product brands—to great success!

Just as products like Marlboro can restage their brands to excellent effect, so, too, can you restage your career brand with resounding results. Remember to reevaluate each element of your branding statement, and then look at *how* you are presenting yourself to the target. We have found that nearly every one of our clients who has done such revising walks away with a brand that's much stronger than his or her original one. And that means getting a better job ... attaining higher visibility in your present company ... or landing more key clients than you've ever had before!

CHAPTER NINE

Down . . . But Not Out!

Whether you are fired, downsized, restructured, or phased out, the words "It won't be necessary for you to come in tomorrow" are among the most painful in the English language. Chances are you will hear them at least one time in a thirty-year career. In fact, the U.S. Labor Department estimates that nearly 80 percent of all employees will lose at least one job in the course of their careers.

Can having a brand statement actually serve as a kind of career insurance? We vote a resounding "yes." Because we believe that if you have crafted a strong brand statement, you will probably be part of the 20 percent who never hear the words "You're fired." Why is this so? Because you will have married a key skill to the needs of your employer, and, equally as important, you will have a personality that meshes with that of your boss and the organization for which you work. Yet admittedly, there are cases where losing your job has nothing at all to do with your brand statement or how you perform your job. You may have the perfect PBS, are doing splendidly at your post, and then boom! The ax falls. Quite simply, you can lose your job because:

1. Your company moves its base of operations.

2. Your company goes out of business.

3. Your boss wants to give his girlfriend/boyfriend/son/daughter your job.

4. Your job is replaced by automation or other marketplace shifts.

5. Your boss just doesn't like something about you.

Add your own set of variables to this list as you see fit. The point is this: life isn't always fair, and sometimes bad things happen, like losing your job. Indeed it's happened to both authors, but we've lived to tell the tale; so will you.

If you have lost your job for any reason, the first thing you must do before starting a job campaign is to find out if in fact your PBS is on target. It's worth reiterating that just because you've lost your job doesn't mean your branding statement is off balance, and it certainly doesn't mean that you're a bad worker. Pick yourself up, dust yourself off, and get back on that career road. If it's any consolation—and we think it should be—the grand majority of our friends and clients who have been fired have ended up with something much better than they had before. We think you will, too.

Sometimes, of course, we *are* the reason we lose our jobs. Just as our PBS contributes to our success, so, too, can unsupported or incorrect elements of our branding statement be the reason for temporary career setbacks. So if you have lost, or think you are in the process of losing, your job, and you believe that your branding statement isn't quite right, this is the perfect time to reevaluate yours vis-à-vis your ultimate career goals.

EVALUATING YOUR PBS IF YOU'RE JOBLESS

To a large extent, the manner in which you should be evaluating your career situation—and, more specifically, your PBS—coincides with the principles of PBS formation that we discussed previously in this book. That, friends, is the beauty in this system: it works whether you're just out of school, in midcareer, are changing careers, or have been laid off. The route is the same: you must evaluate every element of your Personal Branding Statement to ensure that each element works individually and as part of a cohesive, cogent, winning PBS.

If you've been laid off, fired, downsized, or are otherwise jobless at this time, seize this opportunity to take stock of your career by analyzing your PBS. What you need to do is this:

1. Review your skills set with an eye on your most recent job, as well as those you would like to have.

2. Look at your personality/passion to see if they mesh with your present and targeted jobs. (People change, as do our needs and desires; that's part of the joy of the human condition. This is a fine time to evaluate who you are versus who you were, and who you'd like to be!)

3. Take a good, hard look at your target and/or market needs, both in macro and micro terms. Pinpoint the kinds of companies you want to be working for, as well as the kind of boss whose skills and personality will mesh with or complement yours.

Skills

This is the easiest part of the PBS equation to correct. If you are finding, either by your own calculations or your boss's, that you don't possess quite the right skills to function most effectively in your job—that the necessary skill sets are non-existent, overpromised, or undelivered—it is easy enough to gain them. Take a computer course; brush up on your math; take a new graphics class or a public speaking seminar. Outside of surgery and rocket science, there are few corporate jobs that require out-of-reach skills, and any that you lack can be easily corrected.

John Collier is an example of someone who needed to improve his skill set. To the outside world, John had a plum position in the sales department of a trendy fashion house. Charming, suave, and a former model himself, John sweet-talked his way to super sales figures with even the most hard-boiled department store buyers.

Problem is, that was all that John did well. When it came to follow-through, returns, and other elements of customer service, John's boss called him "an administrative nightmare." "Your sales are the best in the company," she complained, "but your organizational skills are nonexistent, and I've had several complaints on follow-through from several big accounts."

John's professional future was in jeopardy. Initially offended and thinking of quitting on the spot, he then did some thinking, and decided that his salary and perks—plus the parts of his job he liked—weren't worth throwing away just because he didn't like the administrative attention to detail his position entailed.

Which brings us to two important points about skills:

• Sometimes you just don't possess certain skills (e.g., knowledge of a given computer program or new nursing procedures). In this case, the only way to get them is through on-the-job training (if possible within your organization), or through your own extracurricular efforts.

• In other cases, you possess the skills required, but just

don't want to use them. Whether it's in our own careers or in those of our clients, we have seen many cases where people just didn't want to complete certain required elements of their jobs. To which we reply: Sorry, but who ever said life was a picnic? You have two choices here: do what's required of you, or if the tasks required are just too odious, find a new job.

In John's case, it was a combination of the above. John saw the wisdom in doing some extra skill polishing, so he signed up for a course in sales management at the adult extension division of a local university's business school. Not only was he able to turn his administrative abilities around, but his progress was so remarkable that his boss promoted him to sales manager at the next available opportunity.

If you've lost a job because, face it, you lacked the proper skills, or if you want to keep a job that is meaningful and important (or merely a financial necessity) to you, by all means gain the skill or skills required to succeed. It's easier than you think, you'll be making a wonderful impression on your prospective new employers or your boss, and you'll feel great about yourself. (We always do when we change and grow.)

Personality and Passion

The most vital point of information here is whether the issue of "fit" works both ways. From your end, you need to consider if you lost your job partly because of:

- the corporate or organizational culture
- the meaningfulness of the type of business or organization you're in, in relation to your interests
- the attitudes and personalities of your colleagues
- your boss's needs

Fact is, some among us play the corporate political game well, but if kowtowing to your boss and his/her boss isn't your cup of tea, perhaps you're better off working for yourself. In any organization, be it non- or for-profit, a certain amount of gamesmanship is de rigueur. You can actively sabotage your job if you actively ignore your boss's requests, don't deliver results, or refuse to be the requisite cheerleader.

One of our clients firmly believes that she lost her job after failing to show up to her boss's birthday party. "It wasn't the only reason, but it was the clincher," Sue says. "Frankly, I think it irked her that I have a personal life, and the only friends she has are subordinates who are commanded to come to her boring little fêtes."

Does this whole situation sound trivial, or does it sound like Sue is merely finding a scapegoat for her job loss? It oughtn't, and this is corroborated by San Francisco psychologist Dr. Gloria Horsley, who says, "Meeting the emotional needs of someone is every bit as important as meeting their business needs. It's part of the human condition."

Proof positive: few among us have lost or quit our jobs without later expressing shock at our eventual replacements. One friend, a magazine editor, was horrified to learn that her assistant had been named as her successor. Sheena practically spit out through her lockjaw, "I majored in English at Yale, and Bethany majored in God knows what at Pine Mattress Junior College. How could anyone possibly consider us in the same breath?" True enough, but Bethany obviously played Kate, their boss, like a violin, while our friend's excellent job performance wasn't matched by the support of her superior's emotional needs. Depending on your boss, that can include ego stroking, cheerleading, or just plain friendliness, but if you fail to exert these qualities, you're your own worst enemy.

So before you go about seeking a job, first set out to determine what kind of environment you thrive in, and if the duties your job entails are a good fit for you in terms of your interests.

Market Gaps and/or Targets

The third component of your branding bio that you should reexamine if you are presently unemployed is that of market gaps. Use this time as a golden opportunity to evaluate: a) changes in the marketplace that may have occurred (or which you anticipate occurring in the immediate future); and b) new outlets for your skills, or kinds of employers that you may not previously have considered.

We know that this can be a very difficult time — especially if you have a family to support or other intractable financial obligations — and we also know it's easier said than done. But do trust us: the lion's share of people we know (both personally and professionally) who have been forced by job loss to totally reexamine their careers have found exciting new avenues — and rewarding new jobs — they might otherwise never have even begun to think about.

Elaine Strong is a clinical psychologist with a Ph.D and fifteen years' experience. She had spent most of her career in private practice, building a strong clientele, before joining an HMO. As she put it, "Many of my and my colleagues' private patients could no longer afford to see me, since their health maintenance organizations demanded they see their own psychologists, and I could certainly see the writing on the wall."

Unfortunately, after spending nearly five years at an HMO, another trend that Elaine could not have predicted occurred: the organization dropped its mental health benefits altogether. "They were positioning themselves as a 'budget HMO' to large companies, so psychiatric and psychological care were the first things to be dropped."

This was an especially bad time for Dr. Strong, as her husband, a police officer, had been killed in the line of duty just months before. "I actually asked God why all this was happening at once, and what I had ever done to deserve this fate."

That said, Elaine remained a pillar of strength. She had to, for her daughter Katie, who was just six years old, and to show her parents and friends that she was going to make it through these trying times intact. How apt is her name: Elaine Strong is one of the strongest people we know—a quality that is vital in her professional work, as well as in her own relationship with family and friends.

But even the strongest among us lose our bearings during the most troubled times, and Elaine was no exception. "The HMOs are getting rid of psychologists right now, and I just can't regain a thriving private practice by snapping my fingers," she said ruefully. "What on earth am I to do?"

If you are in this position, the first thing to do is to take stock of changes in your own industry. Where are the new jobs being created? Where are they being lost? In what industries and/or locations is job creation taking place? As should be obvious, the time to keep on top of changes in your field is not just after you have lost a job (at which time your first feeling is one of desperation and grasping for straws), but at all times. If we asked you right now to answer the questions above, would you have answers? If so, you're a pro; if not, make this an ongoing priority in managing your career.

Who needs accountants? Which aspects of the field are shrinking, and which are growing? For nurses? An article in *The New York Times* we read just recently informed us that nurses of all kinds are in very short supply, and that even recent graduates are commanding top dollar. But you should delve more deeply than that: Where are nurses' jobs? In big cities, small towns, urban centers, suburbs, or exurban areas? Is there more growth in certain subfields (say, operating room nurses or nurse practitioners)? Are the jobs in hospitals, at HMOs, or in doctors' private offices?

You should monitor the developments in jobs in your field no matter where you live or what field you are in, and this holds true whether you are in the corporate sector or in business for yourself. Not today, not tomorrow, but for every day for the rest of your working life.

What is the best place to find out this information? From:

1. The business section of your daily newspaper.

2. The trade magazines and newsletters in your field. (Every field has at least one "trade," and most have several, no matter how specific or arcane the category of job.)

3. Trade organizations representing your industry.

4. Job reports issued by the Department of Labor (which are reported by *Time, Newsweek, U.S. News & World Report*, and other news magazines, as well as by daily papers of record, such as the *New York Times* and *Los Angeles Times*).

5. Your city or region's business periodicals (such as *South Florida Business Journal* or *Crain's New York Business*).

This evaluation is what we would have worked on with Elaine, had fate not kindly interceded first. One evening, as she was talking with Ken, a colleague of her late husband, Elaine learned that the headquarters of her city's police department was looking for a psychologist to counsel officers who had been wounded in the line of duty, who had been traumatized by seeing their partners injured or killed, or who were suffering from depression or anxiety as a result of their jobs. Elaine's interest was piqued, and Ken was able to refer Elaine to the police chief who was in charge of hiring a psychologist.

In addition to being a top-drawer Ph.D. and having years of superb clinical experience, Elaine had a qualification none of her competition did: a husband who had been killed in the line of duty. Nothing, of course, could ever replace the grave personal loss she had suffered, but when she was offered the job of consulting psychologist, Elaine felt a kind of closeness with Dan and was able to resolve (at least intellectually) the apparent senselessness of his untimely death. It was also a way to explain God's way to her daughter, Katie, who was just old enough to understand that her mother was doing something very important in her life.

A Final Word of Hope

We pray that, unlike Elaine, you do not have to go through a personal tragedy to reevaluate your brand. Indeed, for most of us, losing a job is among the most traumatic life experiences we'll endure. But out of crisis does come opportunity, and if you use your period of unemployment to analyze not merely your brand, but your entire career, we promise great things are at hand. With an open mind and willingness to explore new options, they almost always are.

CHAPTER TEN

Rebranding for Long-Term Success

It happens to the best of us. We think our careers are humming along nicely, life is just grand . . . and then, before we know what hit us, we realize that our careers just aren't as wonderful or fulfilling as they once were. Sometimes the change is due to an obvious factor, like a rigid new boss; other times it's something in ourselves that causes the dissatisfaction or lack of enthusiasm we feel.

Have you:

1. lost interest in your work, even to the point of wondering why you chose your present field in the first place?

2. been passed over for a promotion—once or many times?

3. felt that your skills are no longer appreciated or in demand?

4. seen a drop in your revenues (if you own your business)?

5. been dropped by several long-standing clients (if you're a consultant or in private practice)?

6. spent a lot of time daydreaming about other careers— and maybe a whole different life?

If you answered yes to one or more of the questions above, we believe it is time that you think about rebranding yourself. Not next week, not next year, but *now*. Career satisfaction is life satisfaction, and we're on this Earth for too short a time to dislike what we do. It's bad for your family, bad for your friends, and bad for your health to ride any wave except the one that's the highest, most beautiful one you can.

Both of us know exactly how you feel, because we've both been there before. But here's the good news: you are not alone! In fact, nearly everyone we know has experienced a major job change; and far more often than not, the result for these folks has been resoundingly positive. Change can be scary, but it's almost always for the good.

Whether it's one or many of the above points that apply to you, consider this pivotal point not as a career challenge, but as a life-changing opportunity. This may be a scary time for you, especially if your job is in jeopardy, but by considering this not as a crisis, but as a wake-up call, you may well be on your way to wondrous new things.

Why do such wake-up moments occur? Because:

1. *Technology changes.*

NetSmart's Bernadette Tracy is one of America's most respected consultants in the field of motivational research, but when she first started her company, Bernadette realized that to compete against the long-established survey firms, she had to offer something they could not. The brand she came up with utilized Bernadette's double masters in psychology and marketing.

At the time this covered all possible pieces of the puzzle, for who better to tell their companies what their customers were doing, and why? But advances in technology brought rise to a different kind of consumer base, and Bernadette came to realize early on that her company should have a role in studying Internet consumer behavior.

Through her company, corporate heads now could find an answer to the question, "What can the Internet do for me?" Bernadette achieved her goal of long-term success by extending her brand into an exciting new area without losing sight of what she did best—research.

2. *The world changes.*

Societal changes can bring commensurate new jobs, while other trades and professions become history. There used to be women who worked as chaperones to society girls and ladies traveling alone. Now that society permits women to travel solo without any damage to their reputation, chaperones—like the stagecoaches they once rode on—are gone with the wind.

3. *The economy changes.*

In this country, whole towns have been decimated when manufacturing facilities or auto plants close down or move to places like Mexico. When factory workers have no income, it's only a matter of weeks before dry cleaners, cafés, and other retail establishments feel the pinch—and often only a matter of months before they close for good. Many folks have had to rebrand themselves (probably without knowing this term) because the local, national, or global economy has changed, often without a moment's warning.

4. *Your boss changes.*

We don't know a soul who hasn't experienced this, and we'd guess that neither do you. Hard as you try, there are just times when a new boss doesn't see eye to eye with you, or has his sights set on bringing in old colleagues; in either case, this can often be a no-win situation for you. Don't be the martyr. If you simply cannot perform to a new boss's satisfaction, find a new one, either at your present company or a new establishment, or form your own business and become your own boss.

5. *Your job changes.*

Roy is a makeup artist at a busy New York salon. But recently his boss asked him to spend two hours a day manning the reception desk to cover the receptionist while she was on break or at lunch. Roy didn't like this new use of his time, and quit on the spot. (Luckily, Roy also had an income making up private clients; if you don't have an alternate source of income, you will probably wish to tough it out until you have a new job!)

6. *Your health changes.*

Brianna was a landscape architect who had lived with HIV for six years. When she developed full-blown AIDS, she was no longer able to perform the manual aspects of her job, which required frequent site visitation and hands-on work. Using her skill set, she rebranded herself as a freelance interior designer for a variety of firms.

And the most important reason of all:

7. *You change.*

Kiyo Ohara was that rara avis, a creative merchandising executive who also had an MBA (most design or merchandising people are creative forces without a clear vision of how marketing works). Why, then, did she feel the need to rebrand?

"I had been in fashion since getting my MBA and it was getting a little stale; I was on the lookout for new horizons. And, at the same time, I read the writing on the wall: the fashion apparel business was stagnating, and given the cocooning trend, home furnishings was where all the excitement was headed. But to get into home, I had to rebrand myself to make my skills perfectly apparent to my new target industry."

Because the basic function of a merchandising executive is basically the same in fashion or in home, Kiyo's rebranding was achieved by a simple adjustment in her PBS. Her former brand statement alluded to fashion but in her new one she took out any mention of a specific industry. Kiyo believes that all successful people intuitively analyze their existing brand every couple of years—and we couldn't agree more.

If any of these points—and especially the latter one—is true, now is the time to rebrand yourself. Is it easy? Not always. Scary? Sometimes. Yet we urge you to approach this change in your career (and perhaps your life) with gusto, and for the positive force that it is. It's with good reason that the Chinese ideograms for the words *crisis* and *opportunity* are one and the same!

By the way, it's interesting to note that rebranding is a vital part of every product's life cycle, too. Whether it's because of a crisis situation, too many similar products, changing consumer needs, or simple stagnation, most long-lived products have branded themselves at least once. Trendy products, like Calvin Klein's fragrances and clothing, are always being rebranded by their ad campaigns; cosmetics companies regularly rebrand by changing their models. (Estée Lauder, for example, has had Willow Bay, Paulina Porizkova, and Elizabeth Hurley represent the line to present what the company feels is a face and persona of the moment.)

Even the most workaday products need to be rebranded by their managers to stay ahead of the pack. This can be done through technological advances, repackaging, and repositioning, but the aim remains the same: to keep sales of a product at the optimum by periodically reanalyzing the product's attributes, its "personality," and market gaps. These translate directly to your skills/training, personality/passion, and market needs when you rebrand yourself.

Products need to be rebranded to maintain market share, and you rebrand yourself to keep your "personal profits" going strong. However, there is another, more spiritual reason why you should rebrand yourself, in time of career crisis or just plain dead-end malaise: if you disobey this wake-up call, you will not be as happy, or as fulfilled, as you will be if you heed the call and make a positive change in your career and life. The temporary insecurity of forging new paths is far less damaging than the alternative, that of remaining in a job or career you dislike (or even loathe).

REBRANDING YOURSELF FOR MAXIMUM EFFECT

"Yes, it's time," we hear you say. "I can totally relate to one or more of the people and situations you describe above. In fact, the more that I think about it, the more I realize that I'm long overdue for a rehaul of my personal brand. But how do I find exactly what my new and improved brand is?"

You use exactly the same methodology as when you completed your Brand Assessment Test and put together your brand statement for the first time, adjusting for changes in your career, technology, skill sets, and other circumstances, as discussed above. That is, look at each individual component of your PBS to determine what needs improving, or what new goals you should be focusing on, one by one:

1. Skills and Education

This area is of special importance if your career wake-up call has been precipitated by changes in technology in the world at large. Among the questions you should ask yourself are:

- Is my career stagnating because I lack new skills that are required due to changes in technology or in the way my company does business?
- Am I being passed over for advancement because I don't have a B.A./B.S.? Do I need a master's or doctorate to compete effectively in my chosen field?
- Could I attract new customers if I had additional education or training to complement my existing skill set?
- Is a certain kind of career training, certification, or degree required for the specific career/job I have in mind?
- Can I use my present skills in a new field or endeavor by researching this subarea on my own, without the need for formal education or courses?

An example of a successful rebranding story arrives in the person of Penny Granetti:

New Skills, New Story: Penny Granetti

Because her father died when she was a junior in art college, Penny was forced to drop out of school. Her courses in graphic design allowed her to take a job as a draftsman for a large design firm, but she found that her lack of a degree prevented her from being promoted to an art director's job.

In Penny's case, all the elements of her PBS were in place, except for the skills/training part of the equation. She was as committed as ever to becoming a full-fledged graphic designer (personality and passion) and knew that this was a field that would always be in demand (market gaps), but Penny lacked the formal education required to advance.

Many large companies have full or partial tuition reimbursement as part of their employee benefits plan. Unfortunately, Penny worked for a small company where no tuition payment plan was available to her.

It wasn't easy, but by using her savings in combination with student loans, Penny was able to complete her four-year degree. Along the way, she amassed a splendid portfolio, which, when coupled with the experience she had amassed on the job, made her a strong candidate for a junior designer post. Her strong performance and excellent attitude earned her a nearly automatic promotion in her present company; but Penny was also offered a higher salary at another firm, an offer that she accepted with pride. Today she is still at that firm, where she is a senior art director in charge of several blue-chip client accounts.

Like Penny, you may well need to augment your education to rebrand yourself within your chosen field. Or, if you are seeking to reinvent yourself by entering a totally different field, you may need to start from scratch in terms of schooling or other training required. Neither path is easy (especially if you have family or other off-work commitments), but we know of many folks who are glad they took the hard road given the personal and professional satisfaction they now enjoy.

2. Personality and Passion

While this is the segment of the PBS that initially many of our clients don't pay much attention to, often they give it a different weight just minutes into a career session. When people realize that it is indeed some aspect of their personality that doesn't jibe with their present job, or that their life's passions are nowhere in evidence in their PBS, they begin to

understand why the "P&P" element is so vital to the formu-
lation of a winning brand statement.

Letting Personality and Passions Lead the Way: Mike Ahern

Mike Ahern was an art history major in college, but now he
was a product manager at the world headquarters of a major
bank. Unfortunately, however, Mike more often than not
found himself grumbling about the absurdity and politics of
life in a big corporation, how mediocrity was rewarded more
than brilliance there, and how bored he was with his job.
The only thing Mike could get excited about were his salary
and perks.

This situation continued for a good couple of years before
all that changed one day. Mike made a startling career move:
he quit his high-paying, high-status job, moved to a cheaper
apartment, and started graduate work in psychology.

Mike didn't have the advantage of a Brand Assessment
Test per se, but what he did reflected almost to a tee what
you should do if you're in the process of branding yourself:

• First, he took stock of his *personality* and affinities
versus his present job: "I have a personality that doesn't fit at
all in the corporate world. Some people play the corporate
game beautifully, but I don't enjoy it. Plus I couldn't see the
importance of managing product automation for a bank.

"Finally it struck me: I don't want to work with products,
but with *people*. That was a eureka moment of sorts for me."

• Then Mike considered his *passions*. If you are rebranding, you should do the same by revisiting Section II of your
Brand Assessment Test. But here's one more secret weapon
we advise our clients to employ. It's a very simple yet super-

effective way to determine your loves in life. *Look at the magazines and books you read to see where your passions lie.* This is a test we use with graduating seniors and with senior citizens alike. Do you have music mags on your coffee table? Brides' publications by your bedside? Automotive periodicals all around? Looking at jobs in industries related to your interests is a foolproof guide to what you should be doing to make the most of your career—indeed, your life.

In Mike Ahern's case, he looked around his apartment and saw old copies of *Psychology Today* and almost everything written by Jung, Adler, and Freud. He remembered, with a smile, that he had had most of a psychology minor under his belt during his undergraduate days.

Next, consider what you do to enrich your life outside of work. When Mike thought about this for mere moments, he saw a pattern emerging: he had been volunteering as a counselor for several community health projects during the past few years. A career as a counseling psychologist would be a major career overhaul, but Mike was so excited that he immediately went to the library to research jobs in the field—and called ten schools for catalogs that very day.

Today, Mike Ahern is clinical supervisor of behavioral intervention studies for the San Francisco Department of Health and a therapist in private practice. His success is due to having taken stock of his personality, passions, and personal interests, and then securing the required education and training to launch his career. Like all major career changes, this took great courage—and more than a little bit of faith—but as Mike says: "I can hardly imagine what my life would have been like had I not taken the leap. Nearly every week I counsel a patient to make the positive life changes by making informed decisions and having the courage to see them through . . . and because I've done it myself, I really have practiced what I preach."

3. Market Gaps

It would be nice if we could do whatever we wanted, regardless of whether there was actually a need for our services in the real world. But just as you needed to be realistic in considering marketplace gaps when you initially crafted your Personal Branding Statement, here you need to do so again in developing a revised PBS.

If you are in the corporate sector, it is important that your new brand meet a need, either directed within your present company or without. If you are a freelancer, a consultant, or in private practice, you must be certain that your PBS is attractive to a strong potential customer base (be it individuals, corporations, or both), not just yourself.

Reaching New Markets: Ron Thomas

Ron had a problem we all wish we had: he was too successful within his brand. Impossible, you say. How can anyone be *too* successful? At the age of thirty-five, Ron was the most successful real estate agent in his office, which was one of the top three firms in Los Angeles. He had sold over seventy properties the previous year, more than six a month! How had he become so successful? Ron had branded himself as *the* real estate person for condominiums in West Hollywood, California. No one knew the condo market like Ron. No one knew how to sell a condo like Ron could . . . and no one knew how to advertise himself like Ron.

"Every month I would spend a couple of thousand dollars in advertising. I would print up and mail ten thousand fliers. I would advertise in all the local papers. My message was simple: 'No one knows the condo market better than Ron Thomas. Whether you're buying or selling, call me.' A few thousand dollars a month sounds like a lot, but I get it back fourfold in new business," Ron explained.

Ron's Personal Branding Statement read:

A superior knowledge of the condominium real estate market and the drive and determination to ensure each client is satisfied with the results (whether buying or selling) make Ron Thomas the best condominium real estate person around.

We loved everything about Ron's brand: A concise message. A niche market where he had gone narrow and deep, (the condo market in West Hollywood). And his message was single minded and easy to understand. "So what's the problem?" we asked.

"I'm too successful," he said sadly. "The problem is that my brand is so successful that everyone thinks of me for condos only. If I want to start making higher commissions I need to start selling higher-priced homes. Yet no one thinks of me when they want to buy or sell a home," Ron lamented. He had a point. He had branded himself into a lucrative but narrow market. Now that he was a master real estate salesman, the only way he could make more money was to rebrand himself. We recommended he take the following steps:

1. *Because Ron was so intrinsically connected with condos in the West Hollywood area, we suggested he move to an office outside the West Hollywood area and focus on a new target audience.* It took Ron five years to build his brand, and it would take him that long to tear it down if he stayed in West Hollywood. The more simple solution was to go after a different target audience, people in a

different geographic area, who were interested in buying houses, not condominiums. Ron agreed and arranged to be transferred to the Beverly Hills office of his real estate firm.

2. With a new target audience in place, Ron needed to change his Personal Branding Statement to better fit his new career goals and correctly position him in the marketplace.

Ron probably would be using many of the same skills he already had in terms of selling houses, but he would also have to gain a few more. For instance, he knew his new target audience would be spending two to five times as much on a house purchase as his old condominium-buyer target audience. We suggested service would probably be more important to these people because they were spending so much more money on the properties they would purchase. Additionally, people would need further proof that Ron would know how to buy or sell their homes. His reputation, awards, and sales record would be more important than before. So the following PBS was drafted:

Ron Thomas sells more properties per year than any other GMK Realty salesperson. Ron has the drive, determination, and experience to ensure each client is satisfied with the results whether they are buying or selling.

And Ron had these proofs of claims to back all this up:

• number one ranking for number of sales at GMK Realty; at least five properties monthly
• over ten years' experience
• strong reputation, among both his clients and other real estate agents.

As you can see, Ron's brand statement has shifted its focus to his past successes. He has a strong claim that he can use to advertise and promote himself. While Ron is the same person as before, the emphasis of who he is as a brand has been shifted based on his new goals. With this new brand statement, he now had to change his marketing strategy as well, which leads us back to our other recommendations for Ron:

3. To have a base of prospects to start with, it would be smart for Ron to do a mailing to his former condo clients. This mailing would announce that Ron was now selling homes, and if former clients wanted to make the step up from condo to home, now was the time and Ron was the real estate agent. If they had had a pleasant experience with Ron (which the vast majority had), they probably would like to work with him again and be happy to know that he was now selling houses. And if they weren't ready to make the move, they could certainly refer Ron to someone who was.

4. Ron should continue his monthly advertising expenditures, but in newspapers that circulated within Beverly Hills only. We even suggested he advertise in magazines such as *Los Angeles* and *Buzz* (two local monthlies) as much for the publicity as for the advertising. We also suggested he continue with his fliers targeting both condo owners who might be ready to move up to a house and people within the boundaries of his new office. Ron needed to change the message of both the advertising and fliers to focus on his new brand statement (Ron Thomas sells more properties than anyone else).

5. Ron needed a new car. Remember, packaging is every bit as important as your skill set. Ron had made a major move from West Hollywood to Beverly Hills. To back up his claim of being a hotshot salesman he needed to look the part, and in real estate in general—and definitely in Beverly Hills—this meant a new foreign car.

As we rebranded Ron to be new and improved, we used tools that worked in the past (advertising, client referrals, etc.), coupled with his track record and years of experience, to provide a reason why new clients should try him. We also went after a different target audience for two reasons: (1) Ron's brand as a condo salesman had been so strong we needed to shift the target audience; and (2) Ron's new goals required a new target audience—those people who wanted to buy or sell a house.

How is Ron's rebranding working? "I haven't started to advertise yet, but my fliers to old clients have gone out with excellent response," Ron says. "People are now asking me to buy houses, not condos."

WHEN MORE THAN ONE BRAND IS THE WAY TO GO

As we stated in the introduction to this book, we believe that in today's world branding is not a luxury, but an absolute necessity to getting ahead. Moreover, we believe this to be true whatever your career and wherever you may live. This is the result of greater professional competition than ever before and the de facto end to the kind of lifetime employment our parents' generation enjoyed.

It is especially important, therefore, for many people to have more than one brand as a kind of arsenal to job security in our new millennium. Whether you are employed in the corporate sector or are out on your own, wearing more than one hat—and having correlating brands—is, for many of you, absolutely key.

Now this isn't always the case, especially in highly technical fields, or those requiring extensive education and/or training. A brain surgeon is a brain surgeon; if you are one, you probably won't need to work as a general practitioner to make ends meet. If you are a plumber or a priest, you, too, can write your own ticket (without having to worry about developing a backup brand) because both of these job categories are finding new workers in short supply.

For many of us, however, this is simply not so. In large part, this is because one of the millennium's megatrends is, somewhat jarringly, this: projects are more important than people. Many employers, large and small, are seeking skill-fillers rather than long-term loyal employees, a scenario Richard Sennett strikingly portrays in his book *The Corrosion of Character*.

We have already introduced you to many folk who have rebranded themselves to find a new job, especially when disaster strikes in the form of a layoff or downsizing. We advise you, too, to have a backup brand in the increasingly likely event that your present position may be eliminated for a reason that is out of your control.

Referring back to your list of skills and passions is a good way to start. Then look at the concrete list of duties and responsibilities in your present job that you amassed while taking the Brand Assessment Test. What other jobs could you fill, or what positions could you create, using the unique set of skills, talents, and interests you have?

We have already shown you how a freelancer—Paul Lauro—had several identities as a writer to keep himself employed at all times.

Recently, a friend of ours in the publishing field was put out of his job due to an international merger. Having recently purchased a house, Alex was in a state of shock. "What's going to become of me?" he implored. "All I can do is sell books, and there are so many of us [who were laid off]."

We empathized with our friend, because what he was

saying was hardly overreaction—he was perfectly correct. Indeed, Alex was torn apart by visions of losing his house and being thrown out on the street, because he was in a market where the jobs had, in one fell swoop, seemingly dried up.

In addition to the scary prospect of not finding a job in his field, we were also scared for Alex's spirit and soul: he is a recovering addict who has worked hard to maintain his sobriety for nearly ten years. In Alex's case, we were scared that he might slip back into drug and alcohol abuse.

So we set up shop immediately and kept Alex so busy he didn't have time to think about anything but finding an alternate brand—and ultimately a job.

What we found in short order is that Alex could do rather more than just sell books. Even if we kept him in the publishing world itself, he could:

- sell allied publishing products (calendars, gift products)
- do sales promotion (ideating displays, special markets, etc.)
- edit specialty books and manage allied product lines
- work for a book distributor
- serve as a buyer for a major chain
- offer his services to the burgeoning world of on-line book buying

Indeed, Alex was far more than just "someone who could sell books." His new, expanded, revised PBS paints him as:

A seasoned executive with fifteen years' experience working in all phases of the publishing industry, from sales to promotion to purchasing and beyond. A Princeton English major whose knowledge of books and allied products is exceeded only by his drive to find new vistas for publishing sales.

Armed with this newfound, expansive PBS, Alex knew that he was not "just a sales representative," but a well-rounded executive who would always have a place in the publishing world, constricted environment or not.

But this was just the start for Alex. Alex could also use all the skills he had amassed in his publishing career to find a job in sales, promotion, or administration outside of that field—*if* he simply changed his brand to:

> A seasoned executive with fifteen years' experience working in all phases of sales, promotion, and purchasing. A Princeton graduate who has helped achieve a 20 percent increase in sales during the past two years.

With a brand statement like this, Alex was no longer "a publishing person"; he was a sales executive who could write his own ticket with industries in many areas. He, like you, would first examine allied fields for the nearest fit. In Alex's case, that would be companies that distribute their products in similar ways, like videos or records, or to the same outlets (bookstores) like diaries, calendars, magazines, and gifts. This alone would produce hundreds of companies at which he could use his sales and promotional talents. Next, Alex would use his list of passions to identify organizations that speak to his soul, and to which he could apply his talents.

It so happens that Alex had written "environmental causes" and "children's charities" among his passions when he took the BAT. "Unfortunately, these organizations don't need salespeople," Alex lamented. "Wait a minute," we shot back. "Maybe not sales reps *per se*, but they sure need fundraisers. Couldn't you do very well making sales pitches for them instead of for a publishing company?"

Alex's eyes lit up immediately. "I never thought of that

before!" he exclaimed. "And you know what—I would get ever so much more satisfaction working for a nonprofit organization than anything else."

In point of fact, that's just what happened. Alex pitched himself to twenty different nonprofits, and currently works for an environmental group . . . and all because he had an alternate brand in his back pocket.

Having more than one brand *is* the way to go in today's world. Thinking about your alternate brands now helps seal your own job security—and for all of us, regardless of who we are and what we do, that's a very safe, good place to be.

REBRANDING FOR A NEW CAREER . . . AND LIFE

The people we profiled in this chapter all had the vision, courage, and perseverance to rebrand themselves and make positive changes in their careers and lives. Both of us authors have, too. It isn't always easy—in fact, it rarely is—but rebranding can make a major change in your world.

Life is too short, friends, to do anything but explore our dreams, both in our personal and professional lives. We don't know a single solitary soul who has regretted the sometimes painful process of "going for it," whether it's a career on the fast track or on a slower route to personal fulfillment. Once you have used the techniques we have discussed in this chapter to rebrand yourself, you're halfway there, with all the confidence your newfound self-knowledge brings.

A Brand-New You!

Ten years ago, when we'd just come out of school and entered the marketing arena, *branding* was still an insider's term, a word uttered exclusively by product managers and ad agency execs. Today branding has crept into the lexicon of businesspeople in all fields, and it's just a matter of time before it leaps into the vernacular, too.

We couldn't help but smile as, the very day we sat down to write this sendoff chapter, we saw the headline STRUT-TING THEIR OWN STUFF on the first page of the *New York Times* business section. The article, which deals with the trend of department stores' success with private-label clothing, contains this classic line from Joseph Feczko, senior vice president of marketing at Federated Department Stores: "Before [private labeling] was a commodity opportunity. *Now, we are building brands with a personality.*" [italics ours]

After all, if designers like Calvin Klein and Ralph Lauren have brands that have become virtual empires, shouldn't department stores get in on the act? Upmarket emporia like Bergdorf Goodman and Barney's already have such distinctly posh personalities—brands—that even their private-label merchandise holds sway. And if The Gap can create a hugely important international brand, surely even midrange department stores can do the same.

But it won't happen in an automatic or magical way. In order to brand themselves successfully, department stores will have to follow the same formula we have prescribed for you:

Skills + Personality/Passion + Market Needs = Brand Statement

Though the personality Joseph Feczko mentioned is important, it is not all-important, and you know why: because it's got to be a brand someone *wants*. In this case, it would mean identifying an underserved consumer base—say, the midrange middle class suburbanites who can't afford Saks but want something with more panache than Kmart—and creating a personality that is appealing to its target customers. (Focus groups were important for your brand development, and they're even more so for big companies that will spend millions of advertising dollars to promote their new brands.)

Yes, branding is more important than ever, even in industries and practices in which it would have been unthinkable a generation ago. Doctors advertising? Computers with personality? Long-distance phone companies with attitude? You see it every day, along with the thousands of other brand messages we're bombarded with over the television, in print, on-line, and on the air.

Branding. It all started with manufacturers trying to outsell their competitors' bars of soap, and soon became standard operating procedure as companies came to realize that to succeed big-time, you need to stand apart from the pack.

And so do you. In today's hypercompetitive times, a college degree, a trade, or technical expertise alone are no guarantees of a successful career. Instead, like Ron Thomas, the condo—and now home!—real estate agent; Kay Crain, the social worker who is an expert at helping families cope with diabetes; Karen Tina Harrison (the "Beauty Editor Who Wears Makeup"); Mike Beer, the smart founder of the Room Exchange; and like the many other super self-branders we've met here, you need more than talent and hard work to reach the top; you need to carve a professional personality that marries your skills with the market's needs. You need to forge a brand. And if you've followed our clients' stories, spent time with the Brand Assessment Test, and convinced yourself you're the best, we sincerely believe you can do just that.

Success!

David Andrusia

Rick Haskins

David Andrusia, a career coach and marketing consultant, is the author of *The Perfect Pitch: How to Sell Yourself for Today's Job Market* and twelve other books. Formerly head of marketing for New Line Cinema's video group, he also helped establish international brands at Revlon and Swatch Watch USA. A graduate of Columbia and the Sorbonne, he holds a master's from the University of Pennsylvania's Annenberg School for Communication.

Rick Haskins has over sixteen years' marketing and branding experience working as a brand manager for Procter & Gamble and vice president of marketing for the Walt Disney Company. He is in high demand as a brand and marketing consultant for a broad spectrum of clients ranging from Fortune 500 companies to entrepreneurial start-ups. Additionally, he is a guest lecturer and one-on-one career consultant on how to brand yourself.

For more information on seminars, public appearances,
and individual career consulting sessions,
please contact David Andrusia@MindSpring.com